"The book is written with honesty and humor in clear and concise language. Tresa's story is one of compassion, forgiveness, and daring to dream. Letting go of our story that keeps us stuck is the key to creating a new future."

—LILI PARKER, *designer, artist*

"Reading this book confirmed how important Tresa is in my life as a coach, mentor, and friend. Showing her vulnerability confirms that I'm glad I work with her. Her style is relatable.It's like she's in the room talking with you. Simply put, I've reinvented my life by following her steps so I know you can too."

—MICHELLE KAPLAN, *Director of Organizational Development*

"I have worked with Tresa over the last two years. She has consistently challenged and supported me in reinventing myself in my work and life. She is insightful, skilled, and courageous. Her book is full of personal and client stories that show the path to reinvention is doable. If you're looking for someone who can help you pursue your next chapter, look no further. You've found Her."

—PAULA CHRONISER, *President, Chronister & Associates*

"*REINVENTING HER* is beautifully written. I didn't want to put it down. It is highly motivational, bold and is easily relatable. The Reinvention Pillars are contagious and the exercises provocative. You can trust Tresa Leftenant to show you it is possible to go from nothing to having it all."

—CINDY D. WHITMER, *Executive Director, All Faith Counseling Center*

"*Reinventing Her* brings together, with laser focus, what is missing in many books geared toward self-improvement and that is heart, mind, and soul. Tresa Leftenant doesn't ignore the distilled essence of becoming whole in order to move forward as a complete woman."

—ROSE KLEIN, *Founder of Giving Chicks and reinvention expert*

Reinventing
HER

Reinventing HER

HELPING WOMEN PLAN, PURSUE, AND CAPITALIZE ON THEIR NEXT CHAPTER

TRESA LEFTENANT, CFP®

Cover Design by: Amanda Schoolfield
Interior Design by: Beth Fountain Ink.

Writing Coach/Editor: Kathy Sparrow
Copyeditor: Jennifer Carter, Inked! Editing

Because of the dynamic nature of the Internet, any web addresses or links contained in this book may have changed since publication and no longer be valid. The views expressed in this book are solely that of the author and do not necessarily reflect that of the publisher, and the publisher hereby disclaims any responsibility for them.

The author of this book does not dispense medical advice or prescribe the use of any technique as a form of treatment for physical, emotional, or medical problems without the advice of a physician, either directly or indirectly. The intent of the author is only to offer information of a general nature to help you in your quest for emotional and spiritual well-being. In the event you use any of the information in this book for yourself, which is your constitutional right, the author and the publisher assume no responsibility for your actions.

Tresa Leftenant is a licensed financial advisor with LPL Financial. Securities and advisory services offered through LPL Financial, a registered investment advisor. Member FINRA/SIPC. For a list of states where Tresa is registered to do business, please visit www.myfinancialdesign.com.

Certified Financial Planner Board of Standards Inc. owns the certification marks CFPR and CERTIFIED FINANCIAL PLANNER in the U.S., which it awards to individuals who successfully complete CFP Board's initial and ongoing certification.

ISBN-13: 978-0-9903584-0-4

DEDICATION

To Seal Team Self-Esteem—my daughters Alexis and Gina and my son Graham, who are pursuing their dreams in earnest, Elliot who keeps us all grounded with laughter, Paul our angel who keeps us humble and grateful, and Gordon who is indeed the wind beneath my wings—your belief in me has given me flight and I love you with all my heart.

CONTENTS

Reinventing Her

HELPING WOMEN PLAN, PURSUE, AND CAPITALIZE ON THEIR NEXT CHAPTER

PREFACE

I'm going to be honest with you right from the beginning. I'm writing this book to share my philosophy on how to have a happy and abundant life. I'll be turning sixty this year and as I look back, I would say that overall my life has been a journey to the truth. The more I discover what's really true for me, and live from that truth, the happier I become and the better life works for me. The journey to the truth has been called The Hero's Journey, a quest to understand the meaning of life. My journey has provided me the opportunity to understand and discover the meaning of my life, and from that I've developed a personal life philosophy. I will be sharing much of my life philosophy with you in this book—why and how I developed it, and what it has to offer you.

If my life experience is universal, and I believe that it is, any philosophy might include an inner knowing that in order to be happy we must discover our own deep personal truths. We must discover the truth about who we really are and why we are living our life in this time and space. The perspective of living almost sixty years has given me a rearview image of how human beings learn, grow, change, and gain wisdom as each day passes on our journey through life. Our mind, our body, and our spirit blend together in a beautiful symphony of personal truth and expansion. If we are willing to look at what's not working in our lives, and be willing to reinvent ourselves, we will then be able to truly revel in the magic of being alive.

There are over seven billion people on the planet. Many of us have agreed to share certain personal truths of our own as collective truth for all. An example of a collective truth that most people agree upon is that it is better to tell the truth than to lie. Some of us learn this lesson easier and earlier than others. Many of us also disagree, adamantly, on what is considered truth. The current debate over whether gay people should be allowed to marry each other is a good example of the disagreement that takes place over what truth really is. When it comes to truth, we often take sides, believing that my truth is right and your truth is not. I'm not going to try to convince you that my truth is "right." You will sense if elements of my philosophy feel true to you or not. One part of my philosophy is that each of us really knows what is true for us in any given moment, if we are conscious enough to recognize it. If you are meant to learn and grow from what I share in this book, you will recognize if that is true for you. I don't have to encourage you, or push you, or drag you to the knowing. It will be there, or it won't. I invite you to engage in the possibilities that my philosophy offers.

I have reinvented my life several times and in different areas, including how I make a living, the love I share in my relationships, the quality of my health, the way I have fun and restore, and how much financial freedom I have to support my life dreams. We all have infinite possibilities in front of us and when we expand into them, we are given the gift of feeling exquisite joy.

If you are lucky enough to have felt earth-shattering joy, like I have, you can't stop yourself from sharing it and you definitely want to feel it again. A peak life experience overwhelms our circuits in such a mind-blowing way that we just have to talk about it, shout about it, write about it, and invite others to learn how to feel it too! I'm inviting you to join me in reinventing your life so you can experience earth-shattering and exquisite joy as well. Inviting you and teaching you to reinvent your life are peak experiences for me and, believe me, every time my philosophy helps another woman reinvent her life, I am filled with deep gratitude.

In today's world we have unique avenues for sharing our peak experiences. We text, we Tweet, we post on Facebook, we write articles and books, become speakers and coaches, and do just about anything we can think of to attract attention to our experience. We can't keep our peak life experiences inside—we have to share them with anyone and everyone who will listen.

This is what I want to shout, text, Tweet, Facebook, and write this book about. *You can* reinvent your life! *You can* experience exquisite joy! It doesn't matter who you are, where you live, how much money you have or don't have. You have everything you need, already installed inside of you to live the life of your most secret inner dreams. And let's be honest about that. You have those secret dreams. You don't tell too many people about them because, after all, they might tell you that you are crazy.

Let me be the first to break it to you. Well, maybe not the first, but one of many who know that all you need is to give yourself permission to share your *dreams out loud* with me and the rest of the world and you are on your way. I won't tell you your dreams are crazy. I'll tell you they are beautiful and awesome and achievable! *You can have anything you dream of.* All you need to do is get up a little courage, follow a few steps, and like magic—poof—you are living your dream! It's truly possible.

I'm not a famous person. I'm not even known by thousands of people. Well, maybe one thousand, but not tens of thousands... yet. I'm not an Olympic athlete or movie star, a famous speaker or well-known author... yet. I actually think this gives me a lot of credibility. The people in our world who have achieved high places in life deserve our respect and our awe. Many well-known people arrived at where they are today because they had a dream and they pursued it with everything they had. I acknowledge them, but I'm not talking to them. I'm not even inviting you to become one of them. You might and, if you do, I hope it makes you happy.

I'm inviting you, the regular everyday woman to make a decision to follow your dream. No matter how large or small, just pursue it. That's what I did. I had a few dreams, I pursued them, and now I am living them. I dreamed of owning my own business, and now I do. I dreamed of living a romantic novel with a man, and I do. I dreamed of traveling in comfort and style, and I do. I dreamed of creating a happy, healthy, strong body, and now I have one. I dreamed of writing a book and having a national speaking career... and I'm in the process of realizing that dream too! I dreamed of having over a million dollars banked, and I do!

I believe that every woman, every person, is born to live their dreams. I call the process of getting the dream out of your head and into your reality, *reinvention*. The definition on Merriam-Webster.com:

Reinvention is recreating yourself, and aspects of your life, into the expression of your unique and authentic inner self. Reinvention is renewing, reshaping, or reworking your life for the sole purpose of experiencing exquisite joy. Let that sink in for a moment. If you weren't put on this planet to experience exquisite joy, you wouldn't be able to feel it. But you can feel it, and it feels marvelous. Wouldn't it be grand to feel exquisite joy on a regular basis?

"Reinvention: to make as if for the first time something that is already invented, to make or redo completely."

Reinvention also enhances parts of your life that are already on track, but aren't giving you the juice that you know is there but can't seem to access. One woman I acknowledge for showing us how to do that is Sheryl Sandberg, the current Chief Operating Officer of Facebook. Every woman would agree that Sheryl has made it to the top of her career. Now she is sweetening her life by starting a movement to empower women to step into their leadership abilities just as she has. If you haven't read *Lean In: Work, Women, and the Will to Lead*, I highly recommend it. I admire Sheryl because she has provided candid and revealing documentation of her imperfect rise to a position of power and influence. She goes to work every day and embraces a position that few women have the courage to inhabit. From her perch, she can focus on her version of living her dream. Her position could be very lonely, but she has chosen to pay it forward, to share her experience of success with any and all who are willing to listen, and to invite all women to join her on her quest to create a world where women lead from strength, passion, compassion, and confidence. Let's join her. Let's reinvent ourselves into the women that we dream of becoming, living a life that we were born to pursue.

At every level of my own reinvention, I have experienced delicious and unbelievably delightful feelings. When I was in my teens and twenties, when the expression of my feelings had fully kicked in, I did all that I could to turn them down and turn them off. Now, I do all I can to turn those feelings up. Feelings are the truth of our being and when felt fully, provide deep and honest insight into our role in life, our passions, and our purpose for being here. They are designed to reveal the path of our life—to explain its meaning. When you learn how to maximize the wisdom and pleasure provided by your feelings, that's when life gets really good.

My early reinvention attempts didn't go so well, but they did fuel my philosophy and **The Reinvention Blueprint**™ that you will learn in this book. At nineteen, I dropped out of college and moved to California to pursue a career in acting. Falling flat on my face is a well-known expression that clearly underscores this reinvention attempt. I was humiliated by the rough hazing of the movie industry, narrowly escaped being raped by a photographer, was verbally abused daily by my architect boss, was shocked when my gynecologist climbed onto the table and invited me to have an affair, experienced sheer terror when my husband ran away from a black man who he projected was going to attack us, and was horrified by the continual invitation by my husband to have a four-way with another couple. I slowly grasped how unprepared I was to navigate real life—at least real life in Los Angeles in the seventies. After two years of feeling frantic, fearful, and alienated, I left LA, seeking a quieter and saner existence in a small city in Colorado.

There is a saying by Jon Kabat-Zinn that applies to my next reinvention attempt,

> *"Wherever you go, there you are."*

Thinking I could escape the insanity of my life in Los Angeles, I jumped into life in Colorado Springs with renewed energy and hope. I narrowed down my dream of becoming a famous movie actress and settled for acting roles in community theatre productions. Over the next few years, I rose to the top of the acting community, playing the lead role in *All My Sons, Vanities, The Taming of the Shrew,* and other popular plays of the time. I even enjoyed a taste of celebrity, having my name in the local paper regularly, and was invited to interview on local television and radio programs. That part of my life was going well, while my relationships were continuing to crash and burn.

You can take the girl out of the country, but you can't take the country out of the girl. I was still naïve about how to successfully live a life. My marriage was doomed from the beginning and it soon became impossible to ignore. There was a reason a thirty-five-year-old man wanted to marry a nineteen-year-old college student, but I didn't see it until it was almost too late. He was insecure from the beginning about my loyalty and his jealous outbursts eventually became physical. One night he forced me onto the couch and began choking me. My father had controlled me with anger, so I was locked into thinking, "I must deserve this." Luckily, I was able to convince him that I loved him before he snuffed out my life. The next day I moved out. He stalked me for many months, but I was unable to bring any personal power to my ordeal. I allowed my fear to drive me into the arms of another abusive man, who also saw my weakness as an opportunity to dominate me.

Why am I describing these sordid experiences of my early life? Because I want you to realize that the Tresa who is writing a book about how to successfully reinvent life, is the Tresa who started life with limited life skills, no college degree, dysfunctional relationship conditioning, and a very weak will to resist or to succeed.

Life was kicking my ass all over the place and I was letting it happen.

Let's pull the camera back, widen the view, and fast-forward over a few highlights from the next fifteen years. I became pregnant two times by men I couldn't identify and had two abortions before I was twenty-five. I followed my boyfriend to Denver for a better job and started sleeping with another man within a few months. When my boyfriend found out, I left him for the other man, who was handsome, magnetic, and an alcoholic. My best girlfriend became pregnant and, in an effort to hang on to our closeness, I sabotaged my birth control so I could become pregnant too. I married the alcoholic, magnetic boyfriend two weeks before our baby was due and divorced him a year later, only to marry my previous boyfriend a year after that. My life was a series of dysfunctional decisions, motivated by my need for love and approval. I was in denial, hiding from the truth that my life was a mess.

Even as my relationship drama resembled a Jerry Springer episode, my career actually flourished. My father helped me get my first job in high school at the bank he worked for throughout his entire career. The experience I gained from three years of working after school in the proof department served me well, especially when I abandoned college for life as an actress. It turned out that acting didn't pay that well, especially when you aren't getting any jobs. Luckily, I was always able to land a job in a bank. I might have been a bank teller or loan officer, like my father, for the rest of my life if not for an opportunity to interview with a brokerage company. I don't know how I got that job, but getting it may have saved my life. It became the first step on the path of real reinvention. The path that I am on today.

Have you ever seen the movie *Sliding Doors*, starring Gwyneth Paltrow? I consider that first job in financial services as a key sliding door in my life. Taking the job was a pivotal event for me for two reasons. The first reason was because I would not have been offered the job unless I had grown myself enough to be able to handle it. Five years, three years, even one year before the moment it was offered to me, I would not have had the confidence to look the manager of Municipal Bond Trading in the eye and say, "Yes sir, I can do the job." Even though I was shaking and hoping he wouldn't see how afraid I was, I felt deep inside that I could learn the job; I would do whatever it took to keep my word and make him proud. An inner voice told me this was the opportunity of a lifetime and now was the time to jump.

The second reason it was pivotal was that when I walked through that sliding door, I entered a world inhabited by people who were making their life work on a higher level than I was at that time. Soon, I was being mentored by people who lived in expensive houses, who took trips to Europe, who knew what wine to order with dinner, who bought their clothes at expensive boutiques, and who earned high six-figure incomes. I was hired at $1200 a month, but I was motivated, for the first time, to learn what I needed to know in order to eventually have a life like theirs. If not for that door, I may have continued down the path of sleeping with too many men, carving out a living slightly above poverty, and hanging out at the bars with my girl-friends, crying over our beers about how badly our lives were going.

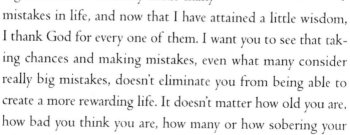

And not only did that door open, I chose to walk through it.

Human beings are incredibly gifted, and we learn what life has to teach us by taking chances and making mistakes. I certainly made many mistakes in life, and now that I have attained a little wisdom, I thank God for every one of them. I want you to see that taking chances and making mistakes, even what many consider really big mistakes, doesn't eliminate you from being able to create a more rewarding life. It doesn't matter how old you are, how bad you think you are, how many or how sobering your mistakes. From the place of human failure, I have reinvented my life, and you can reinvent yours too. I write this book so you will see that reinvention, transformation even, is possible for everyone today. You can learn how to apply what you already have—the gifts you were born with and the talents you have developed—just as I have, for the attainment of your dreams.

If you sense this is true, and if you choose to follow my reinvention philosophy, I will share the tools that you need to reinvent any area of your life. If you are in really bad shape, like I was, you can reinvent ALL of your life. If you learn how to reinvent one area of your life, you can reinvent all areas of your life. And I'll walk you down the path of how it works. As you read this book, the path to reinvention will materialize before you. You'll see how to shift from an abusive relationship to finding your soul mate, from financial scarcity to financial abundance, from obesity to health and fitness. This book will inspire you, surprise you, and invite you to rev up your engine and get moving toward living an exquisitely joyful and incredibly meaningful life.

In the spirit of complete honesty, reinventing your life will require that you be 100% committed to the effort, engaging the steps that I outline in this book. There are several concepts, or philosophies as I call them, which are important to understand before you get started on your personal reinvention journey. I'll also share the Five Reinvention Pillars that capture the foundation for reinvention, as well as The Reinvention Blueprint,™ a simple map of each phase of personal reinvention. The journey will require that you do it for yourself, and it will also require that you have help. I'll show you how to ask for help and how to accept help. By the end of this book, you will know that you *can* reinvent your life and that there are proven steps to follow that will increase your odds of success. When you finish the book, you will connect to the truth that you are living in a time of unlimited possibility—that your life can be an extraordinary life—that you *can* become the woman you are truly meant to become. I invite you to join me as I walk you down the path of **Reinventing Her.**

INTRODUCTION: MY STORY OF REINVENTION

I was driving through an afternoon thunderstorm. The tears flowing down my cheeks matched the raindrops sliding down the window. It was the summer of 1998 and I had just been turned down for a much needed promotion at work. My mounting credit card debt, problems with my deadbeat boyfriend, and my children acting out were overwhelming me with feelings of hopelessness and fear. I pulled over to the side of the road and looked up at the sky through my tears, "Help me out here, God. I don't know what to do. What is it about me that has me experiencing the same problems over and over again in my life?

I moved to Boise, Idaho, in the summer of 1996 after accepting a job as a financial advisor for a regional bank. I left Colorado Springs with hope for a new life after a painful divorce. Moving was my way of escaping the feelings of guilt and shame from my third failed marriage. I had all the same hopes and dreams that every bride has as I walked down the aisle with the man of my dreams four years earlier. Unfortunately, dreams can be smashed in a moment. One morning, I received the call that every person dreads. My husband was at the hospital. He had a car accident as he drove home from an outing with his hiking club. He and two female acquaintances were hit head-on by a family vacationing from India, the father mistakenly driving on the wrong side of the road. The women my husband was driving with were killed and the resulting court case, along with a serious head injury, caused increasing emotional mood swings for my husband. They say that crisis can either bring you closer or pull you apart. At this time in our lives, the latter became our reality.

My life in Boise seemed to go well for a while, on the outside. I was promoted to regional sales manager and the increase in salary allowed me to buy a house of my own. My new job required me to travel around the country, supervising financial advisors and collaborating with other management teams. I felt in over my head much of the time, with the demands of balancing my job and the responsibility of being a single mom with two small children. I coped with feelings of inadequacy and overwhelm by drinking, shopping, and avoiding the truth about my life. I justified my mounting credit card debt with the belief that I **had to have** the best furnishings in my house and a closet full of high-fashion work clothes to prove and sustain my authority at work… and at home.

MY STORY WITH MONEY

This wasn't the first time I overcharged on my credit cards. In fact, it was a habit that became my comfort zone. My relationship with credit began early, when I started working in high school at my father's bank in my hometown of Twin Falls,

Idaho. Everyone who worked at the bank received a credit card. I don't remember receiving instructions about how to use it. Soon, I was picking up the check for my friends' burgers and fries, buying presents and gas for their cars, and loaning money—never asking to be paid back. I didn't know it at the time, but this behavior was my way of compensating for a lack of love and attention.

It seemed like my parents' marriage was in trouble my entire upbringing. I was the baby of the family and I felt alone a lot of the time. It was easy to use money to buy friendship and manipulate people to spend time with me. I convinced everyone that I was popular, well dressed, had a lot of money, and could do whatever I wanted. Even before I reached adulthood, I was using credit card debt to create a façade of financial success that wasn't real. My façade helped to cover up my feelings of inadequacy and self-loathing.

I continued to live a secret life during my twenties, thirties, and forties, creating mountains of credit card debt to convince others that I was happy and successful. Many times I had to work extra jobs to make my credit card payments. During one particularly embarrassing time, I worked as vice president of marketing by day and cocktail waitress at the dog track by night. I knew that paying for my lifestyle with credit was wrong, but I couldn't seem to shake the tendency to grab my purse and run to the mall every time I felt bad about myself. What was it that made me continue this self-defeating cycle when I knew in my mind that it was harmful to my family, counterproductive to my goals in life, and totally unnecessary? At the time, I didn't have a clue.

CONNECTING THE DOTS

My mother and father were always in conflict over money. I listened to loud fights over how much debt they had and how they disagreed about where the money should be spent. I told friends that my mother was a "cheapskate" and my father a "spendthrift." As a teenager, I was so mad at them for not buying me better clothes, providing money for school activities, or giving me enough money to hang out and spend money the way my friends did. Having a credit card filled the gap where my needs were never met or attended to during my childhood. I felt like something was "missing" and that it was my parent's responsibility to know what it was and give it to me. It was much later in my life that I came to realize that blaming my parents for everything I didn't like about my life was just a cop-out and that blaming and complaining just made things worse.

My parents' disagreements over money definitely informed the choices I would make as an adult. When children witness emotionally charged events, they cope with the trauma by making up stories about why it happened. The continual arguing and stress about money in our household resulted in my belief that "no matter how hard I try, I will always have a lot of debt." Another belief about money that I decided as a child was that "I have to work really hard to have just a little bit of money." Both of these beliefs became subconscious drivers of my behavior with money, such as shopping and spending more than I earned, and not negotiating for a salary equivalent to my skills and experience.

There were other beliefs and behaviors around money that I observed as a child that colored my adult relationship with money.

We lived in a middle-class neighborhood in a house built by my mother's father. Mom was clever about how she furnished our home, finding furniture on sale and sewing her own curtains. Taking excellent care of everything she owned was a top priority. She worked hard to keep up with the Joneses, which meant my sisters and I had to chip in to maintain our perfectly groomed yard and spotless house. My mother loved to entertain her friends and neighbors perfectly as described by Emily Post, *Family Circle*, and *Good Housekeeping*! I spent every Saturday and Monday during the summers on my knees, cleaning around the toilet with a toothbrush, dusting and vacuuming the furniture, mowing, and weeding the yard. She paid my sisters and me $1.50 a week for our hard labor, which led me to decide that I would always have to work very hard for money. This decision created a cycle of accepting less than I deserved in many areas of my life for decades.

My parents were children of the depression and I can only imagine how hard it was to have less to eat than you really want. Members of "The Greatest Generation" were raised in real scarcity, so it was only natural that they continued to believe that resources were limited and survival was difficult, even when life became easier after World War II. Those of us who were raised by members of "The Greatest Generation" have "scarcity mentality" implanted in our thinking. Even as baby boomers reach levels of wealth and prosperity never dreamed of by our parents, many of us don't feel fulfilled by our success, always striving for more at the expense of our health, family relationships, and potentially the very survival of our way of life.

My self-defeating beliefs about money and resulting cycle with credit card debt took its toll on my life and filled me with fear and anxiety. Psychologists say that we either mimic the behavior we experienced as children, or we rebel and do just the opposite. I favored my father's "spendthrift" mentality and mimicked my mother's habit of using money to create a picture perfect lifestyle of success and happiness to the outside world. Spending money was my drug of choice, anesthetizing the pain of inadequacy that I silently suffered inside. I didn't believe that I had what it took to achieve the real financial success that I was pretending to already have. My mother's message that success came only from backbreaking work informed self-defeating habits—*spend to feel better* and *work 'till you drop haunted my life.*

During those years, in the nineties and living in Boise, I was on a treadmill of spending more to keep up the façade, and needing more income to pay my mounting credit card bills. I kept reaching for the next promotion, and subsequent higher income, to solve my problems. I worked more hours and spent less and less time with my children. I justified my behavior by convincing myself that I was a great role model for hard work and financial achievement. I was in denial on all fronts in my life. My boyfriend was a poor replacement for my children's biological fathers and the growing strife between them when I was at work contributed to my children developing low self-esteem. I walked on egg shells, patching up their quarrels in the evening, convincing myself that the Band-Aid of buying them a new toy or an ice cream was a permanent fix. I just didn't know how to face the unsustainable life path that I was on. It was much easier to ignore my problems.

But that day driving through the rain, when I didn't get that promotion, I did what most people do when they have nowhere else to turn. I cried out for help—without realizing that I'd been receiving help all along. My cry for help led me to the path of self-development. One of the most valuable lessons I learned while attending a weekend workshop concerned a concept regarding how the Universe (another name we use is God, our Higher Power, Source, or Spirit) will attempt to get our attention about choices that are not working in our life. The Universe loves us and will first attempt to get our attention by

"hitting us with a twig." If that doesn't work and we still ignore what's happening, it will accelerate its message by "hitting us with a two by four." If we still refuse to pay attention, it will "drop a house on our head." I began to experience little "twigs" as the Universe attempted to get me to stop the denial and look at what I was creating in my life with my selfish choices.

It's easy to see the twigs and two by fours now, but I was blind to them at the time. My daughter entered junior high in 1998 and began to hang around with the wrong crowd. My son was struggling in grade school, diagnosed with a learning disability. I was in a constant battle with my boyfriend over his unwillingness to work, which led to his bouts of heavy drinking and abusive behavior. I remember having thoughts like, "I have such bad luck," "Why do I always end up with men who won't work?" "Why don't my children just do what I tell them?" "Why doesn't my boss realize my true contribution and give me a raise?" These thoughts only confirmed my victim mentality and excused me from taking any responsibility for my life.

As I was looking up at the sky with tears flowing and the rain pouring, I asked the Universe to help me understand why I kept experiencing the same problems over and over in my life. The sticks and two by fours had not gotten my attention, so a house had been dropped on my head. When I drove to work that day, I expected to receive yet another promotion with a sizeable raise. I had always received every promotion that I had ever applied for, so I expected to this time as well. "How could this happen?" I asked, as I walked to my car after work. "What am I going to do now?"

My problems were always solved with my making more money. In my mind, I had already paid down the credit card debt and taken my family on a lavish vacation. So there I was on the side of the road, feeling a deeper level of shame, guilt, and hopelessness than I had ever felt before. The house had been dropped on my head. The question was whether it would get my attention. Luckily, as I sat in the car crying and thinking, I began to receive the beginning of a new awareness.

I was at the bottom. My usual methods of avoiding the truth had failed and I couldn't see my way out of all of the mess in my life. A new thought began to dawn on me. Since I was the common denominator in all my messes, perhaps it was me that would have to change if I was to have a different life. As I began to feel the truth of that new thought, I said to the Universe, "Ok, I get it. Just show me what to do. I'll do anything to change my life and help my children."

THE EPIPHANY THAT SAVED OUR LIVES

I've never been a particularly religious person. I was raised attending the Episcopal Church, but the lessons taught there didn't seem to stick. It is only looking back, having experienced the sharp right turn that my life took that day, when I began to understand how clear intention attracts divine intervention. I was very clear as I spoke to the Universe that day. I was ready to stop doing whatever it was that was making my life a mess. My intention became clear: my destiny was now in the hands of a Higher Power. I vowed to pay attention, take whatever guidance was given to me, and do my best to integrate it. You might think that this kind of letting go would produce more fear than I already had. Actually, the opposite happened. I felt calm, with a new sense of optimism about the future as I steered my car back onto the road and headed for home.

Less than a week later, I received a brochure, mailed to me by my sister, about a class to help teens learn how to raise their self-esteem. I didn't know much about self-esteem at the time, so I decided to do some research, ready to keep my promise to do anything to help my daughter change the direction of her life.

Around the same time, my boss sent me to a workshop on communication skills (another twig). At the break, I picked up a book on tape called *How to Build High Self-Esteem*, by Jack Canfield. I thought to myself, "This is curious," seeing a book about self-esteem when I was considering a course on the same topic for my daughter. I decided to buy the book in order to understand more. I remember opening the set and pushing the cassette in the car tape player on the way home from the workshop.

I was completely transfixed by the introductory story about a group of modern Buddhists digging up a Golden Buddha that had been under a mountain of dirt for centuries. Jack said that we all have a Golden Buddha hidden inside us, and that self-esteem comes from a love that we develop for the unique talents and gifts that we are born with. He went on to say that a lack of self-esteem is the root of many of our problems, including crime, drug abuse, and living lives that don't reach our potential. This was the first time I ever considered that I might have valuable gifts inside me. Gifts that were unique only to me and that were put there by Spirit to be shared with the rest of the world. Could it be possible that I had low self-esteem too? Could that be the root of my problems with money, men, and parenting?

Over the next few weeks, I listened to my self-esteem tapes, secretly, over and over in my car. With each story of transformation, I felt more hopeful, and Jack's words seemed to be speaking only to me. I enrolled my daughter in the weekend self-esteem class, called "Walkin' the Talk" and taught by Sue Wade, a school friend of my sister. Sue is a gifted woman devoted to helping troubled teens change the direction of their lives. The content of her weekend workshop for teens centered on helping them identify their unique inner gifts and learning valuable success skills for life. The workshop was experiential.

Sue and her team used action-style exercises designed to help kids learn from their experience of themselves. Research indicates that experiential learning increases retention after the workshop and can contribute to enhanced results.

Parents were invited to do a few exercises with our children during the last day of the workshop. As my daughter and I sat knee to knee, looking into each other's eyes, we were guided to speak our fears and hopes for each other out loud. By speaking honestly and courageously to each other, for the first time in a long time, we began to build a new foundation of trust that would serve us well as she transitioned from her teens to adulthood. Gina connected to her inner gifts that weekend and increased her self-esteem. Subsequently, she felt a desire to help other kids who were headed in the wrong direction. She went on to participate in many "Walkin' the Talk" teen weekends as a staff assistant. I believe this workshop was pivotal in giving her the confidence and drive to achieve her dream of becoming a doctor. As I write this in July of 2013, Gina just completed her residency and is a board certified internal medicine doctor. Dr. Rossetti is starting her first job as an associate professor of medicine at a prestigious medical residency program.

The change in my relationship with Gina after the workshop was so dramatic that I tearfully thanked Sue, the facilitator, on the phone several weeks later. I shared with her that I was listening to Jack Canfield's self-esteem book on tape and that it was having a positive impact on my life as well. I was surprised to learn that her teen workshop was based on studies of Jack's work and years of attendance at a weeklong workshop he facilitated every summer in Santa Barbara. I wondered if it was a coincidence that I discovered Jack's book at a seminar and soon met a woman who had learned from him (in Boise, Idaho), or was it the beginning of a series of synchronistic events sent by the Universe at my request?

Not long after my conversation with Sue Wade, my company sent me to a conference in Chicago. There were several main stage speakers and a few breakout sessions that we could attend by choice. As I was reading the bios of the speakers and deciding which sessions to attend, I noticed that one of the speakers mentioned his training with Jack Canfield. I felt a moment of recognition and a strong inclination to attend his lecture. After his talk, I asked the speaker about his experiences learning from Jack. Just like Sue, he described the weeklong training in Santa Barbara as having a profound and positive impact on his life. I decided right then that no matter what it would take, I would be attending that workshop!

I began to see that something new was happening in my life. Since the day I asked for divine assistance, and declared my desire to change, I was receiving messages and opportunities that were guiding me on a completely new life path. I was saying "yes" to these opportunities and beginning to trust my feeling of the rightness of this new path in my heart. It felt like new insights were arriving every day and I was learning how the quality of my life is based on the choices I make. I was beginning to feel more confident that I could actually **create** the life of my dreams.

I attended Jack Canfield's Self-Esteem Facilitating Skills seminar in 1998. I participated in over one hundred exercises designed to increase my self-esteem, and learned how to facilitate those same self-esteem building techniques with other groups. Newly empowered, I now had the courage to ask my boyfriend to move out, as well as help my son with additional learning support. I had asked the Universe for answers and guidance to a better life. It was clear to me then, as it continues to be now, that all we need to do to have our dreams come true, is to be clear about our desire to learn and to pay attention to the opportunities that arrive in our day.

Over the last fifteen years, I've become empowered by attending classes and workshops with many life masters in the area of personal growth and spiritual development. Several of the lessons that helped me reinvent my life, I share with you in this book. The day I asked for help from the Universe, my life began to change. My willingness to be open to life lessons that I needed to learn, led to a healthier relationship with money, my children, my career, and a better life. As my esteem for my unique gifts grew, I no longer needed to keep up the façade of fake wealth and success. I learned to accept the real circumstances of my life, and to learn and implement proven strategies to achieve real financial success. Paying off tens of thousands of dollars in shameful credit card debt gave me new personal power that led me to open my own business, build a seven-figure net worth (and counting), and design programs to empower others to begin their journey to an authentic and prosperous life.

My story wouldn't be complete if I didn't mention the reinvention I enjoy in the rest of my life. As I healed my low self-esteem and learned how to be authentic, honest, and live with integrity, I attracted a relationship with a man who has similar qualities and values. My current husband and I met as graduates of personal development training modeled after Life-spring trainings conducted in California and around the world. In January, we celebrated the beginning of what is truly a blessed relationship that began fourteen years ago. He bought a date with me at a bachelor/bachelorette auction, which we were both guided to attend by what could only be called significant divine guidance. Blessings can show up in ways that we never believe could be possible. It's only when we are open to the possibilities of life that we are guided to these blessings.

Our marriage created a unique family: my two children Gina and Graham, his adopted daughter Alexis, and his brother Paul, a special man with Down Syndrome. When we moved into our first house together, there were five different last names on our mailbox—definitely a real *Modern Family*. During the past fourteen years, our family has grown to love each other as if we share biology. My life is beautiful, fulfilling, and blessed in every way. Remembering all we have shared together as a family brings me to my knees in a prayer of gratitude. When I think back to my frame of mind in that car back in Boise, and how fortunate I am to have made such a massive transformation in my life, more gratitude prayers flow. I am on Jack Canfield's assisting team and bring as many family and friends as I can to his workshops. I have the honor and privilege to give back to the first mentor that arrived in my life, and to support others on their quest for happiness, success, and joy. This book is my opportunity to pay it forward to you and hopefully inspire you to a similar personal journey of self-discovery and reinvention, one that will lead you to the attainment of a much-deserved life of your dreams.

Chapter One

What is Reinvention Really?

CHAPTER ONE
WHAT IS REINVENTION, REALLY?

ELLEN'S STORY

*I*met Ellen when she was sixty, living in a one-bedroom apartment, working for a retail store for minimum wage and caring for her ailing mother every second she wasn't at work. Ellen told me she felt defeated when she thought about her future prospects. Ten years earlier she sold a business in New York in order to move back to Seattle to help her mother. She planned to be in Seattle only a couple of years, but ten years later, her mother still held onto life and needed Ellen's help more every day. The proceeds from the sale of her business had long been spent and now her financial life was in tatters. She had lost confidence in her ability to ever return to a financially secure existence, let alone to a life of living her dreams.

The future she described during our first meeting included a mental picture of working until she dropped, existing paycheck-to-paycheck, barely able to pay her bills, let alone have extra money to enjoy life. Ellen was five years shy of full retirement age, single, and believed she was out of time when it came to creating a financially free retirement.

When Ellen moved back to Seattle to take care of her mother, she had convinced herself that is what she "should" do. She said yes because she felt it was her duty. She wanted to make a positive difference and she also didn't want her family to see her as selfish or uncaring. She ended up living the next ten years from that "should," which resulted in financial scarcity, conflicted relationships with her siblings, and lost confidence in her ability to pick up her life after her mother passed on. Her beliefs were based on conditioning from childhood, which included a very deep belief that she owed it to her family and that she was obligated to sacrifice her life dreams for their needs. When her mother could no longer live independently, she believed her only choice was to drop everything and save the day.

We often make major decisions in life from limited and confused thinking, an unhealthy need for approval, or to see ourselves as a heroine. We don't always make decisions from healthy, well thought-out motivations, but from inner subconscious needs and old habits of thinking. Human beings are ruled by beliefs, which are ideas or principles that we judge to be true. The problem with beliefs is that we routinely believe ideas that are unproven and we do so because of our emotional attachment to them. Throughout history, human beings decided to agree as a group that certain ideas are true. We do this because certain beliefs have become the very foundation of our need to feel safe, and we want to be able to depend on the certainty of the very fabric of our lives.

However, there is hope. We can learn how to make choices from healthy beliefs that we choose for ourselves. We can give ourselves permission to consider our own needs and wants, our own plans for our future, as well as the needs and wants of others. Compromises can be made that will meet everyone's needs—particularly our own.

Ellen believed she was making the choice to move with an open mind and a caring heart. What she didn't consider was the toll it might take on her psyche, family relationships, and financial security. She responded to her families' request without thinking of the long-term consequences to her personally. If she had stopped to consider a few other scenarios for her mother's care, she might have made different choices. She allowed the huge pressure of "should," as well as the complicated relationships with her family, to rush her into a decision.

THE "I SHOULD" VIRUS

I call some of the more questionable group beliefs "belief viruses" because they inflict the entire society. Many of our most cherished and accepted beliefs no longer support our current way of life. If you consider how ideas become out-of-date, it's not too difficult to see how beliefs become stale as well. Ellen was afflicted by a common *belief virus* that many women share. In general, women are raised hearing that they "should" have a particular kind of life or "should" do particular kinds of things in order to be happy. Here are the top ten "shoulds" that I heard growing up:

1. I should get married and be a homemaker.

2. I should learn how to cook, clean, sew, and throw a great dinner party.

3. I should make homemaking a priority over going to college.

4. I should keep my opinions to myself.

5. I should be thin as a rail and always look beautiful.

6. I should not have sex with a man before marriage.

7. Once I'm married, I should only have sex to create children. (Yup)

8. I should ignore my own feelings and always make sure the other person feels good.

9. I should make less money than my husband, or any man.

10. I should always say something nice, even when I don't want to.

How did these "shoulds" impact my life? I married my first husband at nineteen. I was way too young to know what marriage was all about and how to choose a husband who shared my values and view of life. I have spent many exhausting hours cleaning, cooking, and making sure everything was perfect before I ever invited anyone into my house. In fact, if it wasn't perfect, you weren't invited. I have gained and lost the same five to ten pounds every year of my life, mercilessly punishing myself in the process. I spent decades hating my body and hating myself as I pursued ways of thinking and behaving that weren't me at all!

I could go on, but you get the picture. I allowed "should" messages to screw up my life until I consciously and systematically changed my thinking to support what I truly want to do, be, and have in my life. I create my happiness by discontinuing the control that "should" messages have on my life. If you do nothing else to reinvent your life, investigate and change the "should" thinking that is interfering with your life and happiness.

How many times do you find yourself asking a question that starts with "should" so someone else can take the responsibility for your life because you won't?

- Should I quit my job or should I keep working even though I'm unappreciated, underpaid, and unhappy?

- Should I buy a new car even though I can't afford it?

- Should I invite my cousin to the party even though I don't really like her?

- Should I stay with my husband even though we have grown apart?

- Should I follow the Paleo, Atkins, Weight Watchers, or Dr. Oz diet?

- Should I keep reading this book? (Yes is the answer to that question)

We operate from "should" beliefs all the time in our life, and we pass them onto others by giving advice, often unsolicited, which perpetuates "should" living in our whole society. We want everyone in our life to look, act, and be just like us, and we want to look, act, and be just like them. It makes us feel accepted and we like to feel a part of the crowd. We feel safer when everything is familiar to us. We tell our girlfriend she should wear green because that's our favorite color, we tell our daughter she should marry a wealthy man because we worry she won't be able to support herself, we tell our mother she should take Vitamin D because we heard it prevents Alzheimer's, we tell our broker she should buy index funds because our co-worker told us how much money she made in index funds, and we tell our sister she should quit her job because we are jealous that she makes more money than we do.

Can you see how perilous "should" living can be? When we pass along "should," we often don't realize the inner thinking that is motivating us to say what we say. Because we live a "should life," we believe everyone else "should" too. Having a "should" mentality and passing it on to others just perpetuates a culture where people ignore the inner whisperings of their soul and let other people design their life. Is that what you really want?

It's no wonder we are unhappy. We don't trust ourselves, don't take time to consider what we really want, don't analyze our personal values so they can guide our choices. We don't want to be seen as different, don't want to be laughed at, or ridiculed or judged in any way. We are too lazy, too addicted to approval, and unwilling to step outside our comfort zone. We choose to live a life of compromise because we look around and see everyone else doing the same thing. We think that's all there is to life, that we have no other choice, that we just have to accept things as they are. This is not the case. You can learn who you really are, stand up for your dreams, and

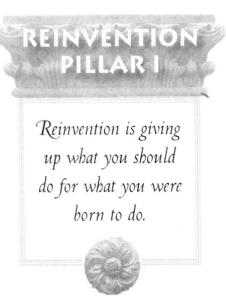

REINVENTION PILLAR I

Reinvention is giving up what you should do for what you were born to do.

make choices that create an authentic joyful life. All you have to do is decide that's what you really want.

When it comes to reinventing your life, I invite you to send your "shoulds" to the basement. And leave them there. *Forever.* I know this is easier said than done because our culture and our parents send powerful "should" messages that are difficult to ignore. We watch thousands of hours of television commercials every year and that's why we have the BMW convertible in the garage and struggle to pay the $750 payment every month. We let our life happen to us because we are unconscious to the messages, and then we complain that we don't have any power to change things!

Stop letting the subliminal messages from society control your life. Install your own messages into your subconscious of how you really want to live your life and who you really want to be. You are in control of what you think. What you think decides what you do and how you feel. You are in charge. You just have to realize it and do some work to connect the dots between what you think, what you want, and what you create in your life.

THE "I'M BROKEN" VIRUS

Ellen had another common belief virus called the "I'm broken" virus. Along the same lines of "I should," she allowed all the mistakes she made in her life to convince her that she was broken in some way. Ellen saw normal life mistakes as losses; her marriage was a loss, her miscarriage was a loss, her business was a loss, and her financial instability was definitely a loss. In her mind, if she had all these losses in her life, there must be something wrong with her. She must be broken and her life

> *Shoulds are trapping you in a life you despise. Reinvention is creating the life you love!*

must be broken. If her life is broken, then she must have to fix it. If she has to fix it, she has to believe she can. But if she is broken, she doesn't believe she can. Do you see the self-fulfilling prophecy of this limiting belief? We go around in circles when we believe we are broken and our life needs to be fixed.

I'm not saying that mistakes and events in life don't feel like a loss and are therefore frustrating and very painful. Certainly the loss of a marriage is a very painful loss, in many ways. What is risky about seeing the unfortunate events that happen to us as a loss, or as a mistake, is that it perpetuates a belief that these things can "break" us. When we feel "broken," or see our life as broken, it's difficult to see the possibility of a new future or that we could indeed have a life filled with joy.

So many women walk around believing they are broken by incidents that happened in their lives. They wear their

"I'm broken" belief as a badge of honor. They hold onto their past experiences and make them into their identity. They bring up their rape or their divorce or the disease that they had ten years ago within the first five minutes of a conversation. They want your sympathy and your attention to control what you think about them. They also use the "I'm broken" badge as a way to keep life on hold and use as an excuse for not being or having more in life. These women have been hurt, and they don't want to take any chances that it might happen again. This virus is the way they keep from reinventing their lives and remain languishing in the comfort of being a victim.

Are you one of these women?

If you are, I am very sorry for whatever pain you have suffered in your life. Life isn't always fair,, and it may not make any sense why it happened to you. Still… what I know about you is that you are strong and capable, and you can handle anything that has happened to you or is happening to you, or might still happen to you. You can survive and thrive no matter what. And what will help you thrive is to square your shoulders, step into your power, and start reinventing your life. Don't let that pain control you anymore! Let it go, send it to the basement! You just have to believe in yourself again. And you will… believe in yourself. All it takes is the choice to do it!

No matter what is happening, no matter how bad it is, no matter how much you are suffering, you and your life are not broken. Even if you had horrific things happen to you in the past, or painful things happening right now, you are not broken. You may believe you are broken but that doesn't make it true.

JUST BECAUSE YOU THINK IT, DOESN'T MAKE IT TRUE.

We have up to 60,000 thoughts a day. Over 98% are believed to be the same ones we had yesterday and over 80% of them are potentially negative. Don't believe me? I invite you to test it in your own life. Watch your thoughts for a few days and see if that is true for you. Because of our conditioning, we have a tendency to see our lives from a glass half empty perspective. We see the problems in our lives more often than we see what is working for us. When you choose to believe that you are broken, you block new opportunities that might be in front of you right now— opportunities that will likely improve the quality of your life right now!

It may seem impossible, but you don't have to stay stuck with limited thinking and continuously making excuses. **You** don't have to believe that other women can reinvent their lives, but you can't. Stop thinking, "I'm different. I'm broken and this is what my life is supposed to be about." That's thinking like a victim, and you can't reinvent your life if you believe you are a victim. Don't take on "being broken" as a fact of life anymore. If you feel that way about your life, send that thought to the basement too! You can build a room in the basement for all of your limiting beliefs. Go ahead. Throw those limiting thoughts down the stairs, lock them up in the room, and lose the key. You deserve to be happy and free, especially if you have suffered unbelievable pain in your life before this moment. That's my point. That was then and this is now. Now is all you have, and you are the one who decides how now feels. The future is full of possibilities when you let go of the past and make the choice to create your future.

Your job is to blast through those statistics and prove them wrong. Your job is to have at least 80% of positive thoughts and 98% of your total thoughts be fresh and full of new beliefs that the next phase of your life is just beginning and it is going to be fantastic!

Once you let go of the past and make the choice that you are no longer going to let it wreck your future, you'll find reinvention is straightforward and so much fun! Reinvent your life from the inside out, living from your passions, your purpose, and your authentic gifts. Instead of focusing on what's behind you, focus on what's ahead of you. That's where happiness resides— in authentically living your life as it naturally evolves and the future becomes right now.

What is "authentic living," you might ask? Psychologists have referred to authenticity as living one's life according to the desires of our inner being, rather than from the demands of society or our programming in childhood. Socrates is reported to have said, "The unexamined life is not worth living." That's exactly what I've been saying! A massive personal growth industry has evolved around the pursuit of happiness, discovery of self, and achieving an authentically lived existence. My mother used to say, "Join the bandwagon." That's one "should" message that I agree with! Come on—join the bandwagon!

I happily join the bandwagon of books, workshops, coaching, and spiritual teachings that broadcast a multitude of invitations to open your life to conscious and joyful living. I invite you to reinvent your life to be more genuine, one that is in harmony with your values, your preferences, your talents, and strengths. Learn who you are and embrace it fully. Be transparent and vulnerable, allowing others to wonder at your beauty, your scars, your innocence, and your journey. Share your beautiful mistakes with others so they will see how they have shaped and taught you and the wisdom they left behind. Be free and choose what makes you happy, letting go of any thought that you "should" make another happy first. Embrace your imperfection and revel in the humor of your differences. Be strong when others disagree with you, be purposeful and resilient, and commit to a never-ending pursuit of your goals. And when you do, you'll find peace, contentment, passion, and energy. Have your mind blown and blow another's mind. Live fully and completely, inspired, and in love with your life. When it is time for your passing, fall to it with grace and gratitude for all that you have been, known, and shared.

ELLEN'S REINVENTION

We often look back over our life and wish for what could have been. "If I'd only known then what I know now" gives us a bittersweet feeling as we contemplate just how we could have done better.

It does take an act of will to convince ourselves that what **did** happen is enough, that it **was** perfect, that we wouldn't have wanted it to be different, even if we could have done or been better. In Ellen's case, after she had some time and distance to contemplate the ten years she spent caring for her mother, she said she definitely wouldn't have wanted it to be different in any way. The closeness and intimacy of caring for a parent became a priceless memory that she will always cherish: the long hours they shared over thoughts and feelings about life, the vulnerability she experienced from her mother as she bathed and clothed her every day, and the way they laughed together in the awkward moments and funny missteps. It's the real life moments that she will remember instead of the judgmental commentary about those moments that she had running through her mind constantly. Caring for her mother changed her, empowered her, and softened her. This part of her story helped her grow into what she needed to be in order to create her next chapter.

Even though the stress of caring for her mother caused Ellen to feel troubled, discouraged, and lose hope, she wanted to believe there was more for her, and when the time was right, she sought help. I was able to help her see her strength, convince her that she still had time, and assisted her in creating a plan to reinvent her life. I reminded her of who she really was and showed her how to set the course of her life in motion so she could experience the possibilities still open for her. Ellen knew deep in her heart that she could turn her life around and once she had my help, she was the one who made it happen.

Through our work together, Ellen slowly changed her mind from believing "It's all over for me" to "My next phase of life is just beginning!" Together, we formulated a new life vision for Ellen. She left out the "should," healed the places where she felt "broken," and began to see the possibilities in front of her. She wrote down her own version of a meaningful and exquisite life, capturing specific goals and action steps that would manifest her vision. She systematically changed her beliefs to new positive thoughts that supported her vision.

Along the way, she experienced doubt, unexpected emotions, and concern from friends and family who worried that she was taking risks inappropriate for her age. With every step she took, new limiting thoughts and beliefs surfaced. She diligently processed where they came from, lovingly let them go, and built a new stronger framework of "I can do it" thinking. Ellen kept reinforcing her belief that she could do it. She didn't resist when doubts came up, but allowed them to teach her where she still had work to do. Every win made her stronger; with every new breakthrough she felt more confident. She never gave up on herself and she never will again. She now knows that reinvention is her life, and that whatever is created will be wondrous, beautiful, and real.

How has Ellen's life changed and how has she reinvented herself? Ellen's passion has always been art. As a young woman, she studied at the best art schools in the country, owned two art businesses, and met and worked with many talented and successful people in the national art world. She longed to get back to her roots, and even though she felt that her talent was rusty and her relationships cold, she asked for guidance on how to find her way to her next evolution.

Divine guidance answered with meaningful signs to move to an art community in the Southwest. She traveled there twice, to feel whether its energy was welcoming, and to investigate if she could make a life for herself there. The Universe gave her an astounding yes by presenting opportunities for her to meet just the right people. The options placed in front of her were so synchronistic that just the right job and just the right place to live literally jumped into her lap! She had one last hurdle to jump before she was free to begin living out her new life dreams.

Ellen had sixty years of history neatly organized in her apartment and a storage unit. She had constructed shrines to the events of her past. Her photo albums neatly chronicled her life. She saved her wedding rings and gifts from marriages that didn't work out, weavings, artwork, and clothes from her two businesses, letters from former lovers. She kept it all because she was afraid that if she didn't, it would mean her life never happened. All of the stuff and mementos proved that she had a life, a good life, and letting it all go was the hardest thing she could ever imagine.

She squared her shoulders and began to really investigate why she kept all of those things. She realized that it was just another "should" message from society and her mother. She had to admit that she hadn't even looked at most of the stuff in her storage unit for over twenty years! If that was true, how could she believe that those things really meant anything to her? As she packed each memento lovingly away, she realized that at one time they had meant something to her, but now it was different. She had changed. Now they didn't mean the same thing to her. Holding on to mementos of her past communicated to the Universe, and her spirit, that she wanted to stay connected to her past. As long as she stayed connected to her past, she wouldn't be able to move forward to her future. She realized she had to let it all go, and even though it would be painful to do so, it was the key to her reinvention.

As she went through every box, read every letter and card, lovingly touched every piece of fabric, she cried and reminisced, allowing each memory to wash over and through her. And then she kissed her memories goodbye, loaded up her car, and hauled it all to the Goodwill and the trash. Trip after trip, box after box, Ellen let her past fall away. It was cathartic beyond belief and healing beyond measure. She consciously and intentionally unburdened her spirit from the garbage of her past. It was exhausting, it was arduous, it was overwhelming, and it was exhilarating. She released the bounds that held her in an uninspired and unfulfilled life. She did it, and then she flew off, free to pursue her next chapter and the promise of an extraordinary new life!

Reinventing You

Helping Ellen reinvent her life was one of the true pleasures of my life. I would like to help you do the same—at least get you started thinking about the Reinvention Pillars. Complete the following exercise in order to consider how Pillar I applies to you.

Take a moment to remember your top ten "shoulds" from childhood. Write them down. How are you living from the beliefs that keep you in an uninspired life? How would letting go of your "shoulds" pave the path for your next chapter?

One of the most meaningful parts to Ellen's reinvention was to let go of the items in her storage unit. She was holding on to them in order to stay connected to her past. Once she let them go, she felt free and had the energy she needed to create her future. How are you making shrines to your past and allowing them to keep you stuck in this chapter of your life? Contemplate how lightening up your environment could set you free to create a new and better life. What will you do? By when will you do it?

Chapter Two

Explore Who You Really Are

CHAPTER TWO
EXPLORE WHO YOU REALLY ARE

As Ellen's story teaches us, everything we think is a belief, and our beliefs grow and evolve from our past and how other people influence our lives. Beliefs define us, they give us an identity; they are like handles that we hold on to when the seas of life get rough. We have more beliefs than we can count and our beliefs can either help us or hinder us. They can support the attainment of our dreams, or they can limit our progress. In this section, I'm going to share my beliefs about who we really are. It isn't necessary to take on my beliefs entirely in order to reinvent yourself, however, understanding them will help you navigate my reinvention system.

How would I answer the question "Who are we, really?" I believe we are spiritual beings living in a human body in pursuit of the full expression of our authentic self. Do you resonate with this idea, or does it bring up resistance or a judgmental thought? Use this opportunity to focus on the feelings in your body. See if you can identify what you are feeling and do your best to interpret it. Perhaps it's tightness in your chest that feels something like anxiety. Perhaps it's a ball in your stomach that feels like excitement. Regardless of your interpretation, it's important for you to notice it. Reinvention requires increasing your awareness of your body, your reactions, your judgments, and your emotions, allowing them to reveal who you really are. In order to reinvent your life, you need to be willing to explore who you are on the inside so you can gain a better understanding of your behavior on the outside—just like Ellen did.

We Think What We Are. . .

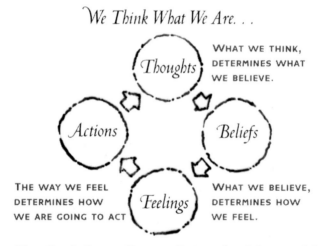

WHAT WE THINK, DETERMINES WHAT WE BELIEVE.

WHAT WE BELIEVE, DETERMINES HOW WE FEEL.

THE WAY WE FEEL DETERMINES HOW WE ARE GOING TO ACT

Thoughts

Actions

Beliefs

Feelings

You Can't Live a Positive Life with a Negative Mind

What we think, determines what we believe. What we believe, determines how we feel. The way we feel, influences how we act, which creates a different thought, and it goes on and on inside our head. Whether you are having a good time or bad time in life is determined by your negative thoughts or your positive thoughts. You can't live a positive life, or create one, from a negative mind. In reinvention, we learn how to observe our thoughts and how they are tied to our beliefs, our feelings, and resulting behavior. Your reinvention begins with what you think. My suggestion that we are spiritual beings is based on a positive belief, and it creates feelings of safety, peace, love, and connection in my body, which motivates me to write books and articles, speak to groups, and coach women and couples to reinvent their life to one of purpose, passion, and authenticity.

Notice that I mentioned the feelings I have in my body. We are not *just* spiritual beings, although that is quite an exciting notion. We also enjoy an equally exciting reality in that we have a physical body. It is through our body that we receive valuable guidance and wisdom from our spirit. It's very nice to have a body, but you are not your body. Not *only* your body. You have a personality, but you are not your personality. You have beliefs, but you are not your beliefs. You have a body, a personality, beliefs, thoughts, and yet, you are not only those things. You are more than that. All of the many parts of you combine together to make you unique, special, and one of a kind. You **are** one of a kind and your life can be one of a kind too.

The word *spiritual* is used commonly in the New Age thought movement. Believers advocate that we are in a New Age, that we are experiencing heightened spiritual consciousness and social and personal transformation around the world. In the United States, the New Age movement grew during the 1970s and 1980s through teachings of various religious and spiritual groups, based on ancient Eastern religious traditions and understanding. The word *spirituality* is often used in popular culture to express New Age ideas, including meditation, natural healing therapies, organic foods, and sacred practices, among others.

Reinvention incorporates many of these ideas and practices that are now accepted by people from all walks of life.

My reinvention that began in my forties has been influenced by teachings of the New Age movement. When I asked the Universe to help me, it was proof that I believed there was a Higher Power. You may have already integrated many of these concepts and practices into your life. I've noticed much of this thinking has crept into television commercials, lyrics in popular songs, and dinner conversations around the country. It may be an easy leap for you to embrace my belief that we are spiritual beings living a human life. If you do agree with the concept, even a little, then you are already seeking reinvention and personal transformation. If you are reading this book, you are exploring whether you are up to that task.

YOU HAVE THE POTENTIAL TO REINVENT YOUR LIFE

The good news is that just like Ellen and me, you are up to the task of reinventing your life, if that is what you seek. You have the potential to reinvent any or all areas of your life. You already have everything required for what you need, right inside of you. All you have to do is set your intention for what you want to create and apply what you have to it's unfolding. One way to check to see if this is true is to look around and notice other people who are already on the path to reinvention. You might see your spouse reinventing his life by going to the gym every morning. You might see your boss reinventing her life by systematically learning her bosses' job so she is ready for it when he retires. You might see your daughter, who has loved cooking since she was three, reinventing her life by going to college at night for a business degree so she can open a restaurant. You see successful reinventions and potential reinventions all around you. Are you having difficulty seeing the same potential in yourself?

Although we gladly support others, women often need permission to pursue their reinvention. One of our most ingrained belief viruses is that if we focus on our own dreams we are being egotistical and selfish. Women regularly put the pursuit of our dreams last on the to-do list. Why do we do that? Growing up, I was punished when I asked for things for myself and praised when I gave to others. I took great pride in the fact that I was a "giver," that I put everyone else's comfort and happiness before my own. Then I woke up. I woke up to the fact that my life sucked, that I was unhappy and dissatisfied from rarely getting what I wanted. It took a strong intention, and a lot of practice, to give myself permission to want. It took an even bigger effort to begin seriously pursuing my dreams. If you are hearing your own story as I tell mine, take heart. It will take diligence in the beginning, but you can learn to ask for what you want, make a plan to pursue your dreams, and still love and support the important people in your life.

We've been conditioned to believe that we don't deserve a better life. It's common knowledge that a high number of women suffer from low self-esteem, but it shows up in reinvention as an inability to take action because of our feelings of inadequacy. We have been taught for generations that our happiness "should" be gained from giving and supporting others. We have been taught that we are the support system that holds everything together. If we were to take the lead, what would our male-dominated society do? We give up our own reinvention because we are reminded that without us to bear and raise the children, cook the food, clean the house, and tell our men how strong and brave they are, the entire world would just fall apart. I'm not saying that doing these things is bad—if we want to do them. And I'm not saying we shouldn't support the men in our lives. Everyone needs love and encouragement—just not at the expense of our own happiness. I'm surprised at how easily this belief virus gets passed down from mother to daughter, decade by decade. In the sixty years I've been alive, I thought there would be more progress. There has been progress, but not as much as I thought there would be, or believe there could be.

Frankly, I'm a bit tired of that message. Especially because I know it isn't true. The world wouldn't fall apart if we let up on the gas a little with the expectations of child bearing, cooking, and cleaning. In fact, women have talents and abilities that go way beyond the hearth. The question is whether or not you are tired of the message to stay in the background. If you are, then it's time to take the lead and go after what you want... and as Sheryl Sandberg says, just lean into it.

If you're ready to go after what you want, say, "Yes, I'm tired of sacrificing my reinvention, my life, because I am afraid to upset the apple cart of generations of outdated and dysfunctional beliefs about the role I'm supposed to play in life. I make this declaration right here and right now. I am willing to let other people judge me, become angry with me, or even reject me in order to have the life I deserve. After all, what other people think of me is none of my business. My business is to live up to my potential. My business is to expand into more of my authentic self every day. That is my spiritual journey. That is what I was born to do. To become who I really am, the unique, authentic being that inhabits my body and has a message to impart and a purpose to contribute. That is what I declare and that is what I'm going to do."

Wow, that felt good, didn't it?

IS SEEING BELIEVING
OR IS BELIEVING SEEING?

You are a spiritual being having a human experience. I know it might be hard to believe because you can't see your spirit. Let's explore that idea for a moment. Is seeing our spirit necessary to believe it is there, or do we need to believe it is there in order to see it; Or feel it; Or know it? Our body is designed with five senses that help us interpret and experience and enjoy our life. We see our hand, we hear our voice, we smell our perfume, we touch our spouse, and we taste our food. What we believe about ourselves, and the world around us, is confirmed by our five senses. However, there is a sixth sense that many women don't put to good use. Our sixth sense can confirm the existence of our spirit and the enormous possibilities that exist for us when we live a spiritually connected life.

In *Trusting Your Vibes: Secret Tools for Six-Sensory Living* by Sonia Choquette, we learn that our sixth, or psychic sense, is not a physical sense like the other five, but is connected to our body and centered in the heart. "Just as our physical senses keep our body informed and directed, our sixth sense's primary function is to

guide our soul's growth and keep us connected to our Source...
who directs us on our path and purpose," explains Sonia.

Another word for our sixth sense is intuition. Our intuition is felt through our body, those bursts of energy that get our attention and seem to carry a message from our Higher Power. In order to reinvent yourself, you will need to develop your sixth sense and explore your connection to your Creator. You will need to learn how to feel it in your body, interpret what it means, and apply it to your life. I teach several ways to develop your intuitive ability in my The Reinvention Blueprint,™ by raising your awareness of what it feels like and when it arrives in your day, which is just one of the reasons to be aware of your body and your feelings—to feel your intuition. Reading Sonia Choquette's books will also help you learn how to integrate sixth-sensory living into your reinvention journey.

My belief is that my spirit came into my body at the moment of my first breath, and that I am a part of the entire divine system that we call God or Creator. I believe that we are all connected on our human journey because we have a small piece of the Creator inside of us, which is called our spirit. Because we are all connected, we are responsible for taking care of each other. I believe that God is outside of us and within us and that human beings were given free will in order to create all that has been created before and all that will be created in the future.

We are the very essence of creative ability. We have all the tools necessary to create our life and our world already installed by our mysterious Creator. Isn't that great news! All we have to do is remember that this is our purpose, our reason for breath-

EXPLORE WHO YOU REALLY ARE 29

ing and feeling and talking and walking. If you wonder what your purpose in life is, news flash—this is it! Your purpose is to create the world that you want to live in. You and I create the world by thinking it into existence. It's help- ful to take a little action too, but imagining it is the first step. The good news is that free will gives you a choice of what world you choose to create. By using your free will to make a choice, you can reinvent your life if it isn't working as well as you hoped it would.

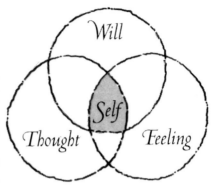

This diagram is from the book *Integral Consciousness and the Future of Evolution* by Steve McIntosh. In his book, various studies of the mind are discussed which support the idea of distinct separate lines of intelligence, and McIntosh proposes that humans have three main domains: Free Will, Thought, and Feeling. He believes the self resides where these three domains intersect. I apply this concept to Reinvention in the following way.

Our Free Will, combined with our mind and our emo- tions, intersect as the expression of our true self as we design our lives and create the world. If what you have expressed and created so far isn't living up to your expectations, then reinvent it. This is why you are here, to continually reinvent your life in pursuit of authenticity and joy! It's fun, it's possible, it's avail- able, it's flexible, it's rewarding, it's loving, and you will notice that it feels really good. That's because when something feels good to you, it's the signal that you are headed in the right direction. If it feels bad to you, it's a signal that you're not. Understanding how we are designed gives us confidence to begin our journey.

Reinvention requires honesty—brutal honesty. The kind of honesty that can break you free from the prison of your current existence, one in which you are likely not living up to your expectations. So let me be honest with you right now. Reinvention also takes courage. It requires the kind of courage that our Creator showed when we ator showed when we

> THE MOMENT YOU TAKE
> **RESPONSIBILITY**
> **FOR EVERYTHING**
> IN YOUR LIFE, IS THE MOMENT
> **YOU CAN CHANGE**
> ANYTHING IN YOUR LIFE

were gifted with our creative abilities in the first place. I mean, take a look. Our Creator took quite a big risk trusting the world to us. I imagine much of what our Creator was hoping for isn't meeting his/her/its expectations either. We are a dismal failure in many ways. And yet, we are also a sublime success in more ways than that. It is all a beautiful, sad, painful, and wonderful experiment. Your choice is how you want to contribute to that experiment. As a recent iPad commercial put it, "Each of us has something to share—a voice, a passion, a perspective. Each of us has the potential to add a stanza to the world's story. What will your verse be?"

Could it really be that simple? Well yes, it can. And it is. It's only those crazy beliefs installed in us earlier in life that muck up such beautiful simplicity.

GIVE YOURSELF PERMISSION
TO DISCOVER YOURSELF

"Why am I holding myself here in this dysfunctional relationship, this over-weight unhealthy body, this financial scarcity? Why am I staying at a job I detest working for a boss I don't respect? Why am I holding myself in a life I don't enjoy? There is an exit door, I see it, but I don't walk through it. What will it take for me to walk through that door so I can reinvent my life?"

Who you really are is on the other side of that door. Symbolically speaking. You say you want to reinvent your life, but you are afraid to take the first step. That's understandable, but there must be something you get for staying where you are. Perhaps it's the attention you receive when you complain about your abusive boyfriend to your girlfriends. There is a lot of pay-off for being a victim. What's the payoff for you? We have a bad habit of complaining about our lives and placing blame on someone or something else. This habitual belief drives an unconscious replay of life as a victim day in and day out. Our victim habit is so engrained in our way of life that it becomes a belief virus as well.

It feels so good to languish in the comfort of zero responsibility. Responsibility takes time and requires energy. We would have to use our brain and figure out what we really want. We would rather be lazy, let life happen to us, and give in to the pull of negative thinking and powerless living. We may be in pain, but at least we are familiar with the pain. We don't see that it really is just a choice we make. We think we have no choice, but in fact, we have dozens of choices, hundreds, even millions. We have so many options to choose from. It's exhausting to even think about it. We'd rather just pretend choice doesn't exist for us, comfortable in our suffering, over on this side of the door. If we were to take even a little more responsibility for our lives, our first choice might be to open our eyes and take a good look around the room.

When we have enough courage to see the truth of what we create out of a lack of responsibility, the door to more choices will magically appear. It's choice that guides us across the room and through the door. It's choice that gets us off our butt and walking across the room through the door and into a journey to an authentic, beautiful, and spiritually connected life. I am being direct with you right now because I want to motivate you to make a choice.

It's a choice to disconnect from the victim conversation that permeates the room. You listen to the news about the problems in our country and you see the exit door clearly. Yet no one is walking through it. That's odd, don't you think? You participate in the conversation about how messed up your company is and how it will never change. Again, you see the exit door; you even point it out to your co-workers. Yet, none of you walk through it. Every day, in every way, your deeply engrained victim beliefs infect you and everyone around you. You see the door and if you would just walk through it, you would feel better, get better, and eventually gain more clarity about your future. But it is so much easier to just take the path of least resistance and stay on this side of the door. It's so much easier to accept your victimhood and justify it by complaining that you don't see the door. After all, there is a lot of company on this side of the door. It looks pretty lonely over there on the other side.

It Takes Courage to Reinvent Your Life, Gobs of Courage

You will need gobs of courage and loads of bravery to walk away from the weight of generations of "societal stuckness" that has you pinned in that room. The good news is that when you get your bravery going, and make the choice to disconnect from that old, decaying, unhealthy belief system, you will be free. You will be *free* to engage your inner beauty, your talents, your installed creative tools to reinvent your life into an outrageous, amazing, super-duper victimless life—a life that your endless, expansive, and ingenious mind is designed to dream up for you. When you grit your teeth, stand up within your Harry Potter vs. Voldemort power, and choose to walk through that door, you will be rewarded. Handsomely rewarded. You will be rewarded with a feeling so enticing, so incredible, so addicting that you will feel yourself swoon. Is there a feeling that could really feel like that all at once, you ask? Yes, there is. It's called Freedom—freedom to live the life of your dreams.

As you go through the door, don't be surprised by the jeers and sneers from your friends as you pass through the crowd. The people you leave standing on the other side of the door will say you are crazy and that you'll be back over to their side soon. They will say you don't have what it takes to become who you are truly meant to be. They will turn away from the door and say they don't care about you anymore. But don't be fooled. They still care about you, even more now that you are on the other side. They are secretly impressed by your courage, by your willingness to love yourself enough to risk it all that they can't keep their eyes off you. They are so envious. They will be watching you like a hawk to see who you become and if you succeed. And when you succeed, the evolution of your spiritual journey, the joy and happiness of your new life, is what will motivate them to walk through the door and join you.

And that's how it's done. That's how we change the world—one person at a time walking through the door to freedom. Patiently, we beckon our friends to come join us. As long as we don't give up and go back over, eventually, they do walk through the door as well. Now isn't that a life purpose worth finding your courage for?

IT'S AN EXCAVATION

In order to disconnect from the victim belief system and walk through the door to your freedom, you will need to do an excavation. Your job is to dig up your beautiful inner spirit that is buried deep inside you. You may not realize it, but she has been hiding for years, and it's time to invite Her to come out. You might have a bit of a challenge finding her, because you buried her long ago, out of fear and pain. You wanted to protect her, because she is your inner beauty, your inner strength, and your inner wisdom. You didn't want anything bad to happen to her, so it's understandable that you buried her deep in the most protected part of yourself.

You buried her because our culture does such a great job at training women to reject their beautiful spirit. Why else do you think we walk around covering up our bodies behind two hundred pounds of unhealthy fat? Why else do we build a mask of happiness and success on the outside, when we are crying and feeling lost and confused on the inside? Why have we allowed ourselves to be convinced that our spirit is actually our biggest flaw and that we must hide our flaw deep down, so deep that for some women, she is never seen or heard from again? Why have we agreed to hide the very part of ourselves that was created to shine, to flow, to invent, and to know?

Why do we continue to hide Her?

We hide her because she has been hurt. Deeply hurt. We have been hurt from the moment we were born up until this moment now. Even though we've already been hurt thousands of times in thousands of ways, we continue to allow others to hurt us more every day. The people who hurt us likely don't mean to, at least not in the way they do. They think they are just getting our attention, or getting us to stop, or getting us to change. They don't really mean to break our heart or crush our spirit, but that's what happens. Our heart is broken into a million pieces every time we are yelled at or swatted or smacked or beat up, every time we are told to shut up, to grow up, to give up, and to bear up. Our spirit is gentle and our bodies are soft, and neither is meant to endure the physical, mental, and emotional pain that human beings hurl at us every day. We are unprepared, on so many levels, to defend ourselves against the onslaught. We shouldn't have to, but we do our best to shelter her, to keep her out of harms way. We bury her behind our mask of busy executive, perfect mom, or selfless volunteer.

Women have been denying the beauty of their inner spirit from the beginning of time. Even when we bury Her and use the cleverest of ways to hide her pain, it still shows through. Other people can see her pain; can sense it behind our mask. In order to reinvent ourselves, we must learn how to heal her pain and let her out of isolation. She is more resilient than you give her credit for. She can be hurt, but she will never be harmed. She can be bruised, but she can never be beaten. She is the strong, powerful, graceful and wise part of you. You are Her, and She is you.

A New Intention to Let Her Shine

You have the opportunity, right now, to set a new intention— an intention to take 100% responsibility for how hurt you are now or will be in the future. You cannot change the past, but in this current moment, you can make a new choice. In this moment, you can choose to set the stage for your glorious reinvention by taking back your power and stopping all the hurt. Today you can empower yourself to teach people how you want—how you deserve—to be treated. Not sometimes, but all the time. You also have the choice to heal the pain from the past and let it go forever. When you lift the heavy boulder of pain that has Her pinned inside, you will have released a strong ally, the most potent piece of you. She is ready to come out, and she is ready to be reinvented.

Your husband, son, boss, or best friend may need "respect-ful-treatment retraining," but in the spirit of total honesty, you have to start with yourself first. You are the one who treats Her the worst. You are the one who needs significant retraining when it comes to loving and respecting yourself. Am I right? Let's make a pact right now, shall we? Let's make a pact that you will no longer hurt yourself in the way that breaks your heart. Let's shake hands and commit to no more throwing up to be thin, no more gluttonous overeating or drinking, no more drugging yourself to sleep, no more yelling at yourself in the car, no more cutting, no more allowing yourself to be hit, no more telling yourself that you are worthless. From this moment forward, you are only going to treat Her with love, with kindness, with the caring and respect that she deserves. You will set the example for your daughters, your sisters, your friends, and your com-munity. You will lead generations of women dedicated to training the following generations of women on how to adore our femininity. Can I depend on you to do that?

When you mess up the presentation at work and beat yourself up about it for two hours lifting weights at the gym, or eating a box of chocolates on your way home from the gym, remember our pact. Treat yourself kindly. This isn't a sprint; it's a marathon. It's progress, not perfection, which we are aiming for. When you fall—and you will—just pick yourself up, drop the chocolates in the trash, and do something really nice for yourself. Sit in the bathtub and feel the water sooth away your cares. On the way to the bathtub, stop and look at yourself squarely in the mirror and say the following, "You are **awesome**. Today you gave an incredible presentation, you helped your mother pay her bills, helped your best friend decide to get a better job, and you kept your word to yourself and went to the gym. You are wonderful just the way you are and I love you with all my heart. Now get in the bath and listen to your favorite music and dream about that handsome guy you are having coffee with next week!" See, you are reinventing your life already!

Your spirit is strong and durable. She will come out of hiding as soon as you allow her to. When you step into your power and take a stand for your life and your dreams, she will be there in a New York second, by your side, in your heart, showing you the way to a beautiful new life. As you take new steps to retrain your mind about how you think and behave in your life, and begin to pay attention to the signs, you will become very aware of Her and how she enhances your life. She is the beautiful way you speak that sounds like a song. She is the excited way you tell your husband about the deep conversation you had with your best friend. She is your reverence for the earth and its creatures. She is your sweet way of expressing love to your children. She is everything wonderful and pure and healthy about you. She may have been hiding for a long time, but now she is out.

Her gifts are so stunning that the rest of us have to shade our eyes when we look at her. Her light shines so bright and her beauty is so encompassing that rediscovering her is the true joy of your life. Living from her beauty and wisdom is the definition of reinvention, and once you are willing to openly love and accept her, it's clear that you and she were meant to be together. She will guide you and protect you and you will do the same for her, a symbiotic relationship of the highest design. Together you will turn toward your future, committed to its enfoldment, determined to face any adversity with strength, confidence, and gobs of courage!

CALMING HER FEAR

The adversity I am speaking of is your fear—your fear of failing, your fear of success, your fear of freedom. The very essence of reinvention is a commitment to continually face your fears. You have big fears and little fears, and fears you aren't even aware of yet. Don't you wish you could wad all of your fears up in a ball and throw them down the stairs? It would be so much more convenient if we didn't have so many fears. Life, and reinvention, would be so much easier, so much more enjoyable.

I am an old man and have known a great many troubles, most of which never happened.

—MARK TWAIN

The truth is we need our fears. We need our fears to let us know when we are in real danger, when we need to perk up and pay attention, when we need to abandon the road we are on all together. There are real threats out there and we are perfectly designed to know which ones are real and which ones are imagined.

Yet, many of the things we fear never happen. Fear really means *fanaticized experiences appearing real*. Fear is another belief virus running amuck in our culture. You are afraid of losing your job, of losing your spouse, of being called stupid, of actually being stupid. You have so many fearful thoughts that it's no wonder you have trouble finding enough courage to reinvent your life. Fear paralyzes us.

JUST BECAUSE YOU FEAR IT, DOESN'T MAKE IT REAL

No matter how many scary monsters your mind can dream up for you, most of them aren't real. They are just that—scary monsters from your childhood—or from something you saw on TV or read in a book. In fact, the very part of our brain that can dream up the life of our dreams is the same part that can also dream up scary monsters and other fantasized experiences that aren't real. You are giving just the thought of something awful permission to scare the heck out of you, enough to stop you from living your dreams. Do you really want to do that? I would never tell you to ignore a scary thought. I want you to check out any and every scary thought that comes into your pretty little head. Then I want you to ask it this question:

> *"Are you warning me about something real or are you just messing with my mind?"*

You might have to ask this question a few times. It might take a little practice listening to the answer to differentiate between real and imagined threats. You may need to ask someone you trust to listen to you talk through your fear before you really know if it is real or not. Perhaps your fear is attempting to get your attention about a part of your life that you are ignoring, like the little twigs that were hitting me on the head before my reinvention. Feelings of fear are great teachers of what's happening in our subconscious. We often jump to a conclusion that our fear is pointing to something obvious in our immediate vicinity, when it's really pointing to past, unprocessed pain that is stubbornly holding us back from living our dreams.

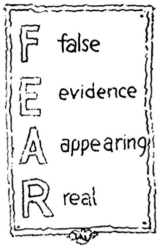

In order to process thoughts and beliefs that are in the way of our reinvention and living an authentically joyful life, we have to be willing to face them, process them, and let them go on **their** time schedule, not ours. Personal growth and transformation require a commitment to pay attention and be brave when something surfaces. And when it does, reach out for help, make an appointment with your therapist or your Reinvention Specialist. Once you make the choice that you are going for it, the more your pain and trauma from the past will want to come up and be processed. You can work to submerge it again, but that will only make it harder to release sometime in the future. You might as well just accept the timing and do the best you can to work through it. The more gobs of courage you have about this, the faster your reinvention will go.

Reinvention expands our comfort zone and is designed to stretch as we grow and evolve. When we take a risk and push through our fear, our comfort zone grows larger. The more we learn to push through our fear, the easier it becomes to grow ourselves. The faster we grow ourselves, the sooner we will attract the life that we aspire to in the future.

OVERCOMING THE BIG PROBLEM

According to Dr. Gay Hendricks, author of *The Big Leap—Conquer your Hidden Fear and Take Life to The Next Level*, the only problem that really holds most of us back is an upper limit problem. "I haven't met a person yet who didn't suffer at least a little bit from it," says Dr. Hendricks, who has counseled hundreds of famous people for forty years on ways to circumvent their upper limit problems. In *The Big Leap*, he describes how the upper limit problem surfaced in his own life and how overcoming it has resulted in a life reinvention where he soars far above his wildest dreams. I describe our upper limit problem this way:

Due to our conditioning, we have a limited tolerance for feeling good or for our life to be going well. We have a fear of feeling happy! When we begin to feel dizzy from the heights of our own success, we manufacture thoughts, feelings, or drama to bring us back down to our comfort zone. We do this in very clever ways. We pick a fight with our spouse, imagine our child having a car accident, convince ourselves that our career is over, and that nobody likes us anyway. *I guess I'll just go home and eat worms.* Now we feel more comfortable. We are very familiar with feelings of dissatisfaction, worry, and hopelessness. They are definitely in our comfort zone. As I've mentioned before, you can't reinvent your life from negative feelings. It just can't be done, no matter how much willpower you apply.

I highly recommend Dr. Hendrick's book, because if you are intent on reinventing your life, you will need some good strategies to overcome your upper limit problem. You are going to experience higher highs than you ever thought possible on your reinvention journey, so you might as well be prepared when your inner fears conspire to send you cascading back to your comfort zone.

THAT DARN COMFORT ZONE!

Just like I encourage you to love yourself, welcome your fear as a friend, and uncover your beautiful spirit, I want you to feel fondness for your comfort zone. I don't want you to get too comfortable with your comfort zone, but I want you to *like* it just the same. You see, your comfort zone is a great measurement of where you are starting from and how much effort and progress you are making on your reinvention journey. Your reinvention—everything you want for your life—currently resides *outside* your comfort zone. You aren't big enough to get what you want yet, even if it is available to you. You have to understand that to begin. You have to grow your comfort zone—grow yourself—in order to be ready for the life you are reinventing. Reinvention is a continual stretching of your comfort zone so it is big enough to encompass whatever you want when it's ready to come into your life.

I look back over my life and see many times when my personal development coincided with an event or goal that I was working to manifest in my life. Once I became aware of this phenomenon, I become intentional about it. The goal I have for myself is in the future. I'm not ready for that future yet, or it would already be in my present. I know in order to have my future, I have to grow myself to be ready for it when it arrives. That means I have to be aware of what my comfort zone is, and the fears that keep me from growing beyond it. What we want has a way of showing up on its own schedule, not on ours, so it's our job to focus on being ready when it does!

Reaching my goals required that I become comfortable with being uncomfortable. As I get better at living outside of my comfort zone, I have raised the level of discomfort that I can live with. The fact is that the more uncomfortable you are, the faster you are growing and the sooner your future will arrive. A great example of this is bungee jumping. For most of us, our fear would scream loud and clear if we jumped off of a bridge, head first. People who are intentional about reinventing their lives and reaching higher and higher levels of success actually use bungee jumping, skydiving, and other adrenalin pumping activities to supercharge their process. After you survive jumping out of an airplane, asking your loan officer for a few hundred thousand dollars to expand your business feels like a piece of cake. I've never jumped out of an airplane, but I have zip-lined in Costa Rica, and it had a similar impact on my ability to go for my goals.

WHAT'S YOUR PUSH TODAY?

Were you told to push yourself as a child? When I wanted to run faster or dance gracefully, I was told by my parents, "You will just have to push yourself, Tresa." It took me years to realize that pushing myself meant I was actually stretching my comfort zone! What a great new awareness! Once you successfully push your-

self, then you've done it, and you can't undo it. You have stretched and whatever you pushed yourself to do is now inside your comfort zone. Now you can look for some other areas to stretch yourself. That's why growing your comfort zone is such a great tool for measuring your progress. The more you push, the more you can push, and the easier it becomes to reinvent your life and the faster you achieve your goals. That is the secret of living a life that you always dreamed of. You get so used to pushing and being uncomfortable, that you push yourself beyond your own imagination. That rocks, doesn't it?

To practice pushing, take it one step at a time. Ask yourself how you will push yourself today. Will you finally ask your co-workers if you can join them for happy hour on Friday night? Perhaps your push is to follow the advice of your best friend and fill out that profile on the dating site. Will your push be to ask your husband to sit down and talk about your financial goals? It doesn't have to be a big push at first, but it does have to make your heart beat a little faster and your breath quicken. Your daily push has to really be outside your comfort zone for it to work. Remember that the goal of your push is to grow yourself into your future dreams. Everything you want is just outside your comfort zone. So let's get started. What's your push today?

WILL YOU OR WON'T YOU?

Many people say there are only two kinds of people: those who won't and those who will. Many people believe every thought they have and never question whether there is more to life. If you are one of those people and you are happy, I congratulate you. Not everyone is meant to live life with their pants on fire, pushing through fears and limiting beliefs in pursuit of a more meaningful life. If reading this section has filled your heart with curious feelings, has brought up more questions than I have answered, and you can't wait to turn the page to see what's next, perhaps you are one of the latter. I hope you are!

One thing I know for sure is that we live from the inside out, either from our limiting beliefs or from our reinvented healthy psychology. No matter what hurts and fears are currently influencing your life, your spirit is whole and healthy and living inside your body. She may have been hurt along the way, but no amount of hurt can truly harm her. She is ready to let go of the past, to see the possibilities in her future, and to stretch her comfort zone so she will be ready to live the life of her dreams. Let's keep going and find out more about Reinventing Her.

Reinventing You

In Pillar II, we created awareness of how we put ourselves aside for everyone else. Now is the time to redirect your energy—to you! Write down your current understanding and beliefs about who you really are and why you are here living in this current time. If you don't have any ideas right away that resonate in your heart, ask your intuition, your inner self, to give you guidance. Take your time with this exercise. There is no need to rush.

Next, consider how you put other people's needs ahead of your own.

What would it take to invite your beautiful inner spirit to the surface and if nothing were in your way?

How would you Reinvent Her?

Chapter Three

Honesty and Truth Telling

CHAPTER THREE
HONESTY AND TRUTH TELLING

*T*here is another simple way to achieve exquisite joy in your life. It is one of the most important secrets to a successful reinvention.

Tell the truth.

Tell the truth 100% of the time. Be honest with yourself and everyone else in your life. Do it with kindness and love and with humility, but do it nonetheless. Stop hiding behind your mask. Let people see the beautiful magnificence of who you really are. Let them see how amazing you are behind the makeup, behind the extra weight, behind the fake smile that is there to convince everyone that you are "Fine, just fine!" They already know you're not, so you might as well own up to it and just tell the truth about it. It will feel so wonderful to let go of all the baggage you carry around trying to convince people you are someone you're not.

There are many different interpretations of what is considered to be "the truth." Most of us are so good at seeing only what we want to see, hearing only what we already believe, saying what we think they want to hear. It's actually quite amazing! I can see something about your life that is right in front of you and you might miss it altogether! I can tell you about something I believe, and you might not even hear me if you believe something different. There is so much more going on with you on the inside than is obvious on the outside.

What is really going on under the surface is your belief system, your self-image, years of conditioning, and a controlling ego—all conspiring to interpret the world in a way that makes sense to you. The way your ego protects you is by giving you misguided mental, physical, and emotional messages through your five senses so you will feel safe and comfortable. The bottom line is that you don't see the world as it really is at all. Not all the time, anyway. This revelation can be very helpful to your reinvention, if you are willing to be open to exploring whether it is true for you. Let me give you an example of how you might be seeing the world from a skewed perspective.

An article on WebMD.com declares a growing body of research that shows coffee drinkers, compared to nondrinkers, are less likely to have Type 2 diabetes, Parkinson's disease, dementia, and have fewer cases of certain cancers, heart rhythm problems, and strokes. At the same time, an article on USAToday.com declares that heavy coffee consumption is associated with a higher death risk in men and women younger than 55. Without going into the details of the debate here, I wonder what side of the debate your beliefs fall into. If you are a coffee drinker, as many of us Starbucks fans in Seattle are, you might tell your friends at dinner tonight the good news about how coffee can protect them from cancer. If you are a tea drinker, like my sisters, you may tell your friends that drinking coffee is hazardous to your health. The question is, can you be certain which report is absolutely true?

In *Trusting Your Vibes*, Sonia Choquette puts it this way, "Most five-sensory people are casual and careless in their observations of the world… their prideful egos draw rapid and erroneous conclusions that lead to all sorts of misunderstandings and failed opportunities."

There is more going on inside and outside of your perception than you could ever think possible. When you make the choice to face your life honestly and choose to be open to who you really are, then your reinvention will flow easily and dependably.

THE CHALLENGE ABOUT THE TRUTH

It's not easy to let your mask of superficiality drop and expose the parts of yourself that you have believed are flawed and broken for your entire life. You have covered up those perceived flaws because you thought that was what you were supposed to do. Once you realize that you aren't broken or flawed, it's essential for you to take steps to drop the mask and learn how to live your life authentically. This is imperative if you desire to live a life of purpose and meaning. I know from my own life that seeking the truth and dropping the mask freed me to create the abundant and joyful life that I gratefully experience now. When I faced how dishonest I was being with money in my forties, I felt overwhelming guilt and shame at first. When I began to understand the inner cause for my outer dysfunction, I started talking about it openly and the shame eventually fell away. I now openly talk about mistakes I make, misconceptions I discover, and imperfections in myself. I have learned, gratefully, that many of us are seeking an impossible level of perfection and most of us are falling short. It's pretty funny if you think about it—we learn from making mistakes and yet we try to pretend that we never make any! Continually telling my story of mistakes helps me remember to give up the pursuit of perfection and to love all the beautiful imperfections that make up "me!"

IT'S THE JOURNEY, NOT THE DESTINATION

She didn't just say that, did she? Yep, I did. I put that overused and well-worn, trite expression right here for you to read and marvel at. It does say it all though, doesn't it? The journey brings joy and fulfillment to our lives. It feels good when we set an intention, take action, overcome adversity, and succeed, doesn't it? It feels good when we watch the video of our zip lining or graduation from art school. We were given the precise emotional reaction needed to fuel us to take the next step, and the next, and the next in our reinvention. Think about it. If we weren't meant to create a better life, we would feel a negative emotion—such as anger, frustration, or sadness—when we win. Instead, when we reach a goal or overcome a limiting belief, most often we feel **fantastic!** It's all designed perfectly.

Remember that you have everything you need to live the life of your dreams, already installed, and all you have to do is learn how to apply what you have to dream-making. Are you beginning to see how it works? It is really so simple! It's a lot of fun too, once you get the hang of it! I just love the truth of it. Do you feel the truth of it inside you?

TRUTH IS A GREAT GUIDE ON YOUR REINVENTION

I watch *American Idol* from time to time because I love watching people be empowered to go for their dreams. I also love feeling empowered to go for my dreams, and I think everyone who watches the show feels the same way. It's one of the most popular shows ever created for television, breaking every record of viewership and ranked the #1 show every year for eight seasons. Isn't this an indication of how human beings crave a more impassioned life? We watch *American Idol* and dream of being in their shoes. Millions of dreamers show up every year at auditions all around the country, hoping for their chance to live their dream. Are you feeling empowered to live your dreams?

When Simon Cowell was one of the judges, he was known for his blunt and often controversial criticisms of contestants. I was always impressed by his honesty. He was willing to say what everyone else wouldn't. He saved many contestants from pursuing a career that they were obviously not suited for. You might not have agreed with his opinion or his style of delivery, but you have to admit that his willingness to take significant heat for speaking his version of the truth was, and is, admirable.

That's just it. We all have some version of the truth. You can find yours through reinvention by committing to uncovering and speaking your truth. Be a beacon of honesty and integrity in your life. Being honest with people may mean you have to suffer through some painful moments, but the pride you feel from doing so is unmatched. Living with integrity is a choice that can fill you with pride, power, clarity, and confidence. There is a price to pay for living and speaking the truth, but the rewards are priceless.

Five years ago, I started a women's discussion circle. My dream was to give all of the members an opportunity to learn more about themselves by discussing topics of interest to women. I encouraged members to speak their truth about each topic at our monthly meeting. At first, we were awkward, exposing our opinions to disagreement or judgment. Eventually we learned that being disagreed with wasn't the end of the world. It actually helped us learn more about ourselves, contributing to higher self-esteem and confident living. Over the years, we've talked about living our values, if love can last, the role of self-esteem in our world, whether we are racist or not, handling difficult family dynamics, when it's ok to lie, social responsibility, women as a force for good in the world, and spirituality versus religion, just to name a few of the fifty plus issues we've taken on. I have to say that the results of my experimental ladies discussion group have far surpassed my wildest dreams.

Members of the group have positively changed their lives by telling the truth. One member discovered a passion for dancing after talking about an unconscious belief with the group. Another worked through a belief that she had to put a family member's needs ahead of her own.

She recently announced her first art show opening and is preparing for another! Another member overcame a fear of public speaking and joined Toastmasters. When we tell the truth about what we are really feeling, what we truly want, it opens the door to creating a plan to achieve it. Without the truth, we often stay locked up in the dark, blind to the possibilities that are right in front of us.

Given my experience facilitating the discussion group, I can confidently report there is a connection between speaking our truth and successful reinvention. The truth helps us get to know who we really are. The truth helps us figure out what is important and what is not. The truth empowers us to take risks, to get out of our comfort zone, to seek new solutions that we have never considered before. Telling the truth and facing the truth is the foundation of reinvention.

OUR AGREEMENTS ABOUT HONESTY

I was raised on the "if you can't say anything nice, don't say anything at all" diet. This belief virus caused me to allow relationships and life to just happen to me. I didn't know how

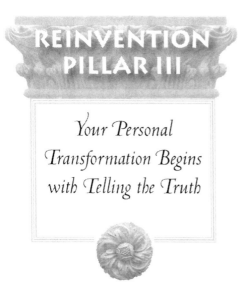

REINVENTION
PILLAR III

Your Personal Transformation Begins with Telling the Truth

to stand up for myself when people bullied me or pushed me into doing something that wasn't right for me. I kept my mouth shut. I spent years in relationships that were both unhappy and unhealthy. It took personal power to learn how to stand in my own truth. Continuing to do so is a challenging part of my journey, but a worthwhile one. Speaking my truth has lost me a few friends, and gained me others. I mourn the loss of anyone who would rather play the "dishonesty game," but I am closer to friends who subscribe to the "honesty game." I've made a choice to no longer compromise speaking my truth in order to have a counterfeit friendship. I seek relationships with real people, imperfect people, people who willingly show me their scars, their pain, and who have learned that it is surviving our failures, not hiding them, that make us whole. Which game are you playing in your relationships?

Another limiting belief that stands in the way of reinvention is the tendency to be an approval seeker. I know this one all too intimately. Seeking approval is often disguised as giving, compromising, and putting everyone else's needs ahead of our own. Seeking approval is how the "dishonesty game" gets embedded in our friendships with women. We know the rules, although they have never been written down or passed on verbally. Girlfriend rules seem to be in our DNA. We just **know** what is expected from these relationships. Here is how the game is played. My job is to listen to everything you say and agree with it. Your job is to do the same for me. We aren't supposed to give each other feedback or question each other's motives or behavior or to offer any advice. My job is to listen to your bullshit and reinforce it through exclamations of horror and shock and "how could she/he" comments. When I do that, you are grateful. You tell me what an amazing friend I am and how much you love me. You give me approval. I go home happy and you are happy, and the bullshit monitor is through the roof.

Did I mention we aren't ever to give advice? Actually, we often give advice, mostly unsolicited advice. We tell our girlfriends how they "should" live their lives. We jump at the opportunity to tell them how they would be so much happier if they did things our way. They pretend to listen but ignore our advice, and we go on with the game, happily and unconsciously sucking up for each other's approval. Have you noticed that men don't play the dishonesty game? Have you noticed that when you get home, full of approval, and tell your partner about how much bullshit your friend just laid on you, that he tilts his head to the side and looks at you with complete wonder in his eyes? He can't understand what you are saying? He can't understand why you are so upset about the dishonesty game. He says, "If my guy friend would have said that to me, which he never would, but if he did, I would just turn to him and say 'that's bullshit Bob.' He would shrug his shoulders and say, 'Yea, you're right' and we would go back to watching the game."

I have to admit it. I have penis envy about this. I want to be a guy with my girlfriends. I want to call their bullshit and then help them figure out a way to make their life better and then go back to watching the game. I'm sick of supporting their bullshit and them supporting mine. I need someone to call bullshit on me, because I'm too blind to see what is obviously right in front of my face. I want to play a new game with my girlfriends. I want to play the honesty game. How about you?

I need my friends to tell me what I can't see because my ego confuses me. I believe what I think about myself and that is exactly what is keeping me stuck where I am. It's not easy to admit that I'll never be a rock star like the ladies on *American Idol*. I need someone to lovingly and kindly tell me that I sing off-key, I'm too old, and would look ridiculous in pink spandex. I need my own female Simon Cowell. Then, she can hold my hand while I mourn the loss of one of my most dearly held lies about myself. Hearing the truth allows me to let it go and get on with discovering what I am meant to share with the world. By the way, I did have designs on being a famous singer earlier in my life and a very courageous friend *did* tell me I was full of shit. I looked at her, frowned, and said, "Thanks for telling me." Then I went back to my job at the bank.

You can't reinvent yourself if you let your ego be in control. Ego is about protecting you and keeping you safe, and if you are going somewhere you've never been before, which is where you are going in reinvention, you won't feel safe. The only way to disengage the control your ego has over you is to tell the truth about yourself. The ego can't compete with the truth. The truth comes from within, it is something you know, and you know it because your Higher Power knows it. That is why reinvention requires a relationship with your inner self and your Higher Power. This is why you need to develop a keen connection to your sixth sense. Once you allow it to, your spirit will take the lead in your reinvention, and you will begin to feel the truth about your purpose and the right path for your life.

A COUPLE OF DOSES OF TRUTH
ABOUT YOUR MONEY

In my financial planning practice, I help women reinvent their relationship with money, and there is no better place to see our ego at work than with our dealings with money. We hear about dishonesty and lack of integrity in our financial system on a daily basis from the media. With this in mind, I invite you to check in with how much blame you place on others for your financial situation. Some people blame the highly paid "Wolves of Wall Street" for the recent chaos in our economy. Other people blame the government or financial advisors. The first dose of honesty that I want to give you is that you are creating it. You are responsible for the chaos, dishonesty, and lack of integrity in our world. You are responsible for the conditions in our economy—at least as much as you don't take a stand, speak up, and say what is true for you. When you avoid responsibility for your own financial situation and allow those who manipulate

INTEGRITY INSPIRES TRUST

our system for their own gain to be in charge, you are contributing to it. By staying uninvolved, you have contributed to the greed, the lying, and the cheating that is rampant in our world. I wish it wasn't true, but it is. Our ego convinces us that to speak up would put us into jeopardy and would be too much risk. In actuality, when we don't speak up, when we don't stand up against dishonesty, we support it. Do you sense there is any truth in what I'm saying?

I know many people who are devoted to taking action and changing the world. If you are one of those people, I salute you. On the other hand, I have observed that many human beings would rather let someone else do the hard work of changing the system. What are you really mad about when you think about our financial system? What are you mad about when you think about your own financial condition? What could you do, right now, to let it be known how you feel? Why do you stop yourself from speaking up and taking action on conditions you don't like? Why do you hold your truth inside and let your life happen to you? In order to reinvent your life, you have to be willing to step outside your comfort zone, speak your truth, and stand up for change. It's you and I who have the power to change what we dislike in our world. We just have to make a choice to take responsibility for it and stop expecting others to do the work for us. We create our world by thinking it into existence. What fabulous new idea do you have that would make our financial system better?

If you see the truth in what I'm saying, then I'll take this discussion one more step. Are you one of the many people who believe that you can't trust financial advisors and that's why you don't have one? We want our financial professionals to be without question in their commitment to integrity, and yet we go into their offices and tell all sorts of lies about our true financial situation. We hide our real level of debt, our lack of understanding about financial markets and the economy, and our unwillingness to stop spending money on things that make us feel better about ourselves but sabotage our dreams. We say we want a budget, but it's a lie, isn't it? We don't want a budget. We want our financial advisor to create miracles for us so we don't have to say no to ourselves. We want them to know exactly when the market is going to go down and to get us the hell out! We **hate** it when we get a statement that reflects a decline. "It's all their fault," you cry. And then you go see another financial advisor and tell them about how bad your current financial advisor is messing up your money. The new financial advisor says they would never do that, so you fire your current financial advisor instead of sitting down and telling them the truth so they can really help you.

We expect a financial plan that will guarantee a future that is worry-free and will keep us spending in the way we have become accustomed to. We want it all and yet we don't provide our planner with real clay from which to mold a realistic plan. We want to reveal the real facts about our money about as much as we want to eat dirt. Our money is just too personal to talk about to anyone. We would rather keep our head in the sand and just keep on bitching. The bitching doesn't help, but at least it feels good.

INTERESTED IN CHANGING THINGS?

Imagine how much more energy you will have if you stop wasting it on telling lies and refusing to face the truth about yourself. If that idea appeals to you, then just be honest about your true financial situation, admit that you don't know what you are doing, and empower yourself to ask for help. Find the advisor that is as committed as you are to 100% honesty and responsibility and hire him/her immediately. Don't wait another minute. Now that you know what it takes, there is no reason to wait. Your financial reinvention has been begging you to get real and get going for a long time.

A reinvention of your financial life requires that you learn to trust yourself and you can't trust yourself as long as you lie to yourself about your real financial situation. You can't trust yourself as long as you don't take responsibility for your life and your future financial results. You can't trust yourself as long as you are out of integrity about how you handle money. Here's the good news. As soon as you choose to walk through the door to freedom, your level of integrity will increase immediately. Your trust in yourself to make better decisions and to choose a path that is right for who you really are, will go up markedly. The more you tell the truth, the more the bullshit meter goes down, and the more the trust meter will go up. Throw in a little stretching out of your comfort zone, a dash of knowing what you really want, and you'll be in that financial advisors' office, asking the right questions with confidence and clarity so fast it will make your head spin.

Bullshit Meter Down, Trust Meter Up, Reinvention Initiated!

It is possible to have a plan that guides you toward your authentic and abundant future. It requires that you be willing to take yourself on in a way that you may never have done before. It requires that you stop bullshitting yourself and the financial advisor and get to work transforming your money based on the truth. If you believe that it's the financial advisor's job to take your money seriously, it is. But it's also your job. If you aren't

trust yourself. you know more than you think you do.

committed to your money and your future, how can you expect them to be? If you aren't committed to taking action and being open about learning and receiving feedback, how can you expect them to be? Breaking down your belief system about money is a course of reinvention that requires your complete and total commitment. That is what it will take for you to achieve financial freedom and have the money you desire, and deserve, to support your next chapter, and the next, and the next. Remember, you have everything you need to change your results with money. I believe in you!

THE DANGER OF STEPPING OVER THE TRUTH

Here is an example of how we unconsciously avoid the truth even as we are receiving signs that could save us from unpleasant consequences.

My clients Bill and Bethann experienced a financial life event few are blessed to go through. They didn't see it as a blessing at first, but now they do. In a moment, you will see why. Bill made a mistake in his business that cost them dearly. It was one of those mistakes that he didn't see coming. He and his business partner, Fred, borrowed $400,000 to open a second lighting store in a neighboring community. The building was completed and the lamps hung when Fred found out his wife Sheila had cancer. It was devastating news and her prognosis wasn't good. Fred and Sheila fought the good fight, but she passed away within a few months. After her death, Fred seemed to have no energy. He couldn't get past his anger over the unfairness of what had happened. Fred began drinking before work and sometimes didn't even show up. Bill tried to be understanding, and to talk to Fred about his grief, but the burden of running two lighting stores was challenging and taking up all of his time, focus, and energy. One day, Fred didn't show up for work again and they couldn't find him for several days. Finally, the police located him in his car in a deep gully. He had driven his car off the road late one night and was killed in the resulting crash.

Bill and Bethann were devastated. They had lost two close friends in less than a year, and the business income from their second store was declining. It was 2008 and the economic collapse wreaked even more havoc on Bill and Bethanns' life. Eventually, they were forced to close the new store due to lack of business, their family home was lost to foreclosure, and the resulting financial consequences were so dire they believed it would take a lifetime to recover.

When I met Bill and Bethann, they were in deep grief and very angry with what had happened to them. They took their anger out on each other. Bill blamed Bethann for not telling him the truth about the real state of their financial situation sooner. Bethann blamed Bill for taking such a big risk by opening a second store in the first place. They both blamed Fred for leaving them in the way he had, and for not being there to help them pay off the debt that they still owed on a store that was no longer functioning.

I could tell that Bill and Bethann were stuck in their anger and blame when they sat down in my office. It wasn't so much that they yelled at each other. Their anger came out in more passive aggressive ways, such as sarcastic comments, defensive accusations, and sullen silences. I was sympathetic to their predicament for sure, and gently guided them through questions designed to help them understand that blaming each other and events beyond their control was not helpful. They couldn't change the past, and if they continued to be unwilling to accept responsibility for their future, I feared more than their financial security would be in jeopardy.

It took some time, but eventually Bill and Bethann accepted their circumstances, and even opened up to the truth of how they contributed to its unfolding. Bill admitted he had felt a strong intuitive message that the community where they built their second store might not be large enough to support it. He ignored those feelings because he was so excited to double their income. Bethann admitted she had also seen danger looming when Sheila told her over lunch one day that Fred was an alcoholic. Bethann promised Sheila that she would never mention their secret. Had Bill known the truth about Fred, he most likely would not have brought him into the business as a partner, or opened the second store.

THE BLESSING OF THE TRUTH

Our work together helped Bill and Bethann process their understandably deep feelings about what had happened to them. Once they were willing to learn how they missed the truths that would have helped them make different choices, they were highly motivated to do the best they could to never step over the truth again. They also uncovered old and limiting beliefs about money that were unconsciously contributing to poor decision-making and conflict in their marriage. This new level of truth telling opened up a channel of true intimacy between them. Once the emotional air was cleared, they could successfully collaborate on a new financial life vision and choose between a number of realistic options to pay off their debt and improve their living situation.

I recently met with Bill and Bethann for their three-month coaching check-in. I was excited and impressed by how much progress they had made together to improve both their financial situation and their relationship. As they reported steps of our plan that had been implemented, I noticed a new tone of respect in their voices. They spoke calmly—with confidence—offering each other a chance to tell the next great news item first. I have to admit that I became misty-eyed listening to them. I was reminded how quickly our inner spirit will jump to our aid with just the smallest invitation. Their spirits were shining through their loving eyes as they smiled at each other. Their whole demeanor was completely different, and I felt how committed they were to this new path. They realize now that their future happiness is completely dependent on them, and they know they are not alone. They have each other and a whole host of talents and skills and inner gifts available to guide them on their reinvention. Bill and Bethann will soon be breaking ground on a new house. Their financial future is bright—all because they were willing to see the truth.

This story illustrates how dangerous it can be to step over the truths in our lives. Bill felt an intuitive hit about the community, but chose to ignore it. Sheila chose not to ask for help, but to ask for secrecy when telling Bethann about Fred's drinking problem. Bethann chose to agree to keep the secret instead of gently encouraging Sheila to ask for help. By ignoring these truths, events were set in motion that caused enormous pain and financial disaster.

Something inside Bill and Bethann urged them to seek help. The fact they were willing to learn from this unfortunate series of events, instead of living in pain and bitterness, can be attributed to the strength of their spirits, and their deep love for one another. There will always be the possibility for sad or catastrophic events in our lives. The question is whether we have the strength of spirit to learn what we are meant to learn and move on to reinvent our next chapter.

THE CHOICE IS YOURS

In each moment, you are confronted with a choice to see the truth, to tell the truth, or not do either. You have likely spent your entire life being unconscious about much of what is going on right in front of you. Avoiding the truth may have contributed to your lack of funds, your lack of fun, and your inability to create the life you wish for. People lie all the time to their friends, their family, their spouse, and their children. They justify lying by believing that they are doing it for the person's own good, when in fact, they are lying for their own misguided reasons. We have convinced ourselves, in certain circumstances, in a lot of circumstances, that lying is better than telling the truth. I admit that telling the truth in the moment can be much harder than avoiding it. We have an unspoken agreement in this culture that lying is ok, as long as we don't tell the truth about it. Pretty crazy belief virus, isn't it?

It's time to find our courage and be willing to not only tell the truth, but to hear the truth, too. It's time to live our life from what's real, what's honest, and what's true. It's time to let go of the façade and to drop the mask. It's time to stop believing that the truth would just be too painful to tell or to hear. It's time to change our thinking about honesty and truth telling. When we lie to one another, we are actually saying that we don't believe either one of us is strong enough to handle the truth! How offensive is that? It's all a mixed up mess of projections and misguided belief systems that has us all trapped in a sort of hell of good intentions and icky feelings. We have made things far too complicated!

Let's make things simple. Tell the truth first. Tell the truth faster. Give it a shot and see what happens. If truth telling doesn't work for you, you can always go back to your "dishonesty game" comfort zone. Once you do commit to truth telling, you will feel the toxins start to clear out of your system immediately. You will shed pounds magically. Your stress will go down.

The University of Notre Dame did a study, "Science of Honesty," to determine if living more honestly actually contributed to better health. Half of the 110 volunteers were instructed to stop telling major lies for ten weeks. The other half received no instructions about lying at all. Both groups were tested every week with health and relationship measurements, in addition to a polygraph test measuring the number of major and minor lies they told that week. Over the ten weeks, the group that was instructed not to lie experienced four fewer mental health complaints, such as tenseness or sadness, and three fewer physical complaints, such as sore throats or headaches, than the control group. The non-lying group also reported that their close personal relationships and overall social interactions had improved, or had gone more smoothly during the week. "Statistical analysis showed that this improvement in relationships significantly accounted for the improvement in health that was associated with less lying," said Lijuan Wang, co-author of the study.

Honesty and truth telling is the foundation of reinvention and conscious living. Now that you see how important it is to your happiness and your health, commit to learning how to do it one step at a time. Slow down. Observe your life and how you function within it. Look at the world around you with fresh perspective. Ask more questions, take more time to understand the answers, and slowly allow your intuition to speak ahead of your ego. She knows the truth and you can trust her. Resist your tendency to blame others for the events in your life. Establish a new habit of inquiry, of assessing the situation with your intelligence, along with your intuition, before you react. Invite your emotions to communicate how you really feel about your life and other people, and listen to its message. Ask your Higher Power to provide you with clues about what you really want.

> *Be honest, brutally honest. That is what's going to maintain relationships.*
>
> —LAURYN HILL

Look intensely for the places in your life where you are wearing blinders. Remember the last time you listened to your girlfriend and thought "she's kidding herself." Where are you kidding yourself? Are you living with someone who has long been sending you signals that he/she has moved on emotionally but not physically? Are you ignoring those signals? Are you kidding yourself about your health? Have you been ignoring signs that you need to see the doctor, but you refuse to let the message in? Where are you kidding yourself about your money? Is it the secret shopping habit every weekend at the mall, or that you tell yourself you'll start saving next month, but next month never comes? Don't forget to ask where you are kidding yourself about playing the "dishonesty game" with your girlfriends. Come on, get real, invite her out for a glass of wine, clear the air, and establish a new "honesty game" together. Make up the rules, write them down, and practice them every day. When you are in your eighties, you can look back and laugh about how ridiculous you were before you started living from your truth.

Reinventing You

Pillar III is about telling your truth. Pick one area of your life where your intuition is telling you it's time to face the truth. Is it your relationship, your health, your money, or your friendships? Grab your journal or go look in the mirror and let the truth, the whole truth and nothing but the truth, come cascading out of you. Start practicing by telling yourself the truth in secret, so that you're ready to tell your truth in public. When you are finished, drive over to your favorite ice cream store and treat yourself to a hot fudge sundae. You deserve it. I'm very proud of you.

Chapter Four

What Do You Really Want?

CHAPTER FOUR
WHAT DO YOU REALLY WANT?

MANDY'S REINVENTION

*M*andy, a woman in her early sixties, told me she had several times in her life where she began a journey to her authentic self and then a life event would throw her off course. When she left her first husband, she had a plan to get more personal power as she never wanted to be in an abusive partnership again, but she continued to struggle with feelings of self-doubt and lack of direction. In her late fifties, she was diagnosed with a rare heart condition. As she was going through the diagnosis process, she thought, "Is this it... is this the end for me?" That truly pushed her through the door to reinventing her life. Mandy attended my workshop, The *Money Madness Cure*, in the fall of 2011. She was also reading self-help books and attending other workshops that were giving her the same message. She was hearing that it was time to empower herself to discover her passions and to design a plan on how to achieve them.

"I've always been trying to do the best I could in life, but in earlier days I was trying to get better or do better for everyone else. I wanted to be that perfect person who would make everybody else in my life happy. I was always doing what they wanted me to do so I would be pleasing to them," Mandy said. "Having the heart condition woke me up to realize that I wanted to find out what made me happy. What I learned was that if I didn't please myself first, then I wouldn't have anything left over to give to the people I loved."

FIRE UP THE DREAM MACHINE

The fun part of reinvention is fantasizing, dreaming, and eventually planning what you truly want in your life. If you are a person who buys lottery tickets, you know exactly what I'm talking about. A lottery ticket buys you an inexpensive pass to dream! Your amazing imagination, another gift from your Higher Power, is your own personal dream machine. You can fire up that dream machine and point it toward any part of your life that needs a little improving. Voila, there are all of your amazing dreams, in full Technicolor, with lights, sound, and all the actors in place. You can dream up anything with your personal dream machine. Whether it's your love life, your work life, or your fun life—the only thing stopping you from making your dreams a reality is a simple choice. Let's see what can happen if you choose to turn on your dream machine!

A ROMANTIC COMEDY

You are running along a beach in the Caribbean, slow motion running with the music of Bolero playing in the background. You look fabulous in your tight one-piece bathing suit (it took eight weeks at the gym to get that tight bod), and your hair braids flow and bounce in the breeze (does this sound familiar somehow?). You look marvelous, perfectly tanned, and as you lose yourself in the feel of the sun and the sea and the music, you suddenly trip over a large piece of wood sticking up out of the sand. You go sprawling headfirst right onto a blanket where Peter, the guy you flirted with last night at the bar, is sunbathing. You are incredibly embarrassed by your clumsiness and as you spit sand out in his face, he points to a huge gash that you have on your shin. You lie back on the sand, getting a lot of it in your bathing suit, and try not to swear or cry out in pain in front of this handsome guy. He just looks at you with panic in his face. Trained lifeguards come running from all directions, and suddenly four incredibly buff men are bent over you with concern on their faces. You smile and before you can utter a word, four sculpted bodies pick you up and carry you (good thing you lost that fifteen pounds) over to a pickup truck parked on the edge of the beach. Everything is happening so fast—you wave to Peter and wonder if you will see him or these guys at the bar later tonight. You notice there is an old smelly mattress in the back of the truck and just as you squeak out "Noooo," they throw your greased, sandy body right on top of it (music stops). Yuck! Well, nothing you can do about it now. You'll take a long shower when you get home (music starts up again). Soon, these four gorgeous men pick you up again and run you into the emergency room at the local clinic. The nurses immediately start cleaning your wound, giving you water and putting an IV in your arm. Within fifteen minutes you are peacefully resting on a soft, clean mattress, and you sigh with relief, beginning to doze into a warm slumber. Suddenly, the curtains are flung apart, your eyes fly open and *he* walks into the room. You stare at one another—it seems like forever—and you feel yourself sit up as if controlled by a strong desire to kiss him. You stop yourself just in time as he leans over your bed and says, "Hi! My name is Dr. Roberts. Who might this beautiful woman be?" And the rest, as they say, is history, hopefully X-rated history. . . fade to black.

POWER SUITS

So now everything is good in the romance department. Let's envision a fabulously lucrative and rewarding career. Dream machine ready? Action!

You step off your private jet and into a waiting limo, where you are chauffeured through the streets of Paris to the largest technology convention in the world. You were recently picked to take over as the first female CEO of the most innovative cloud technology company in the world. You now earn more than 75% of the wolves on Wall Street. Their people now call your people for lunch appointments. As your limo pulls up to the convention center, you step out into the whir of cameras taking your picture as the media and local fans capture the moment and welcome you to town. You are wearing a super tight Donna Karan suit and Giorgio Armani pumps, carrying a Burberry bag. Your entourage of four similarly fit and fabulous ladies, push through the crowd and you enter the hall, just in time to walk on stage to give the keynote speech. The crowd roars to see you in person and then a hush rolls over the crowd as they hang on your every word. International news reporters capture every moment of your speech and rush to be the first to air your cutting edge perspective. Later, you dine with friends in a private and exclusive restaurant where the owner and chef announces a new signature dish named in your honor. . . fade to black.

Romance and career—check! I think you are getting the hang of this. Dream machine ready? Camera focused on fun and recreation!

YOUR LEGACY

You grew up on the East Coast and have always dreamed of owning a beach house on the shore just like the one that you visited in the summers growing up. Your best friend and her family had enjoyed Grandma's house on the ocean for generations and you seemed to fit right in—enjoying the fun and frolic of a carefree summer by the sea. Sitting in your apartment, you sip tea and stare at the fire, remembering all the adventures you shared—building castles in the sand, laughing and playing in the surf, and roasting marshmallows over a fire at night. If only you could pass on these wonderful experiences to your children and grandchildren. Suddenly, your phone rings and it is your friend letting you know that her grandmother passed away peacefully in her sleep at age ninety-nine. You reminisce for a few moments and then she tells you that she and her family members are gathered at the beach house right now. Her brothers and sisters had just been remembering all the good times too, and mentioned how you always hoped to own a house like Grandma's one day. Your friend wanted to let you know that the house next door had just gone on the market, and asked if she should put a deposit down to hold it on your behalf. You squeal with delight and tell her that you are on the next plane. As you hang up the phone and run to pack your bags, you thank God for granting your wish. Even as you throw your suitcase in the car headed for the airport, you are already visualizing all the fun and memories your family will create in your new beach house by the shore.

Wasn't that fun? These life scenarios are only examples of course, a small taste of the possibilities available to you when you engage your dream machine. I'm not assuming that you don't know how to do this. You may already have visualized your dream life and have actual plans in motion to achieve heartfelt desires. If you need a little assistance cranking up your imagination, perhaps my stories will be the ticket you need to see how easy it is and give it a try. Your personal movie may include visions of an once-in-a-lifetime romantic vacation with your husband, opening a cupcake business in your hometown, or volunteering at your local grade school helping kids learn how to read. The trick to a fabulous life vision is to give yourself permission to dream without any limitations. Take away the reasons you tell yourself you can't, stop the voice that tells you "who do you think you are," and just have a little fun. The dream machine is free and it is available 24/7 with unlimited resources to make your life movie as sweeping and memorable as you want. No need to bring reality into it yet. We'll get to that later. But first, you need to tap into your desires.

YOUR "WANTER" IS BROKEN!

Are you someone who just can't seem to get her *wanter* going? Are you someone who cringes at the very thought of imagining a different or better future? Our "wanter" is the part of us who desires, who visualizes something and feels the pull to attain it, the part of us who imagines a better life and feels completely excited by contemplating how to achieve it. Remember, we were born to create our life. We think it into existence. The way we do that is to visualize what we want and then spend our days in pursuit of getting it. We have millions of things we want, some as small as a piece of candy, to as large as becoming a CEO. The danger happens when we follow another person's idea of what we want instead of our own. Just like Mandy, many of us believe we *should* do what other people tell us to do, rather than seek the true path for our lives hidden deep in our heart. When considering a reinvention, it's important to align who you are with what you want.

When I talk to women in my financial planning and coaching practice, I'm amazed at how many women say "I don't know" when I ask them what they want for their lives. They get this far off wide-eyed look on their face and sound a little embarrassed that they don't answer right away. Don't worry if you have experienced a similar moment when someone asks you what you want, and you reply, "I haven't a clue." You are not alone. In fact, you are in very good company. I would venture a guess that more women have a broken "wanter" than have a functioning one.

WHAT'S HOLDING YOU BACK?

We've already discussed my belief that there is nothing broken about you so I'll make a slight correction to my statement—your "wanter" isn't actually broken. It's just disconnected. It has been detached and you are the one who has unhooked it. "Why would I do that?" you ask. There is a very good reason why. In fact, there are several reasons why your "wanter" has been disconnected.

DISCONNECTING OUR "WANTER"

One of the major drivers in our life is wanting. We want all sorts of things and we want them all the time. This wanting that we feel can even get a little tiring. Wanting definitely has consequences. For instance, if you love shoes, your wanting might drive you into a number of shoe stores where you purchase every pair of shoes in sight, eventually running out of money and closet space! This happened to Imelda Marcos, wife of the former President of the Philippines, who reportedly had a collection of over three thousand shoes. If you want to eat every brownie you come across, your pants might get too tight and you would have to buy new ones, again, a risk to your budget. It you want your son to become a lawyer, but he wants to be a musician, you might end up having a quarrel, or worse. There are many inconvenient and uncomfortable consequences that arise from wanting.

Our wants range from wanting to **do** (run a marathon), wanting to **be** (CEO of a private company), or wanting to **have** (a Porsche or house by the beach). Whether we get what we want determines whether we feel great pleasure or significant pain. That is why it's easy to see why you might have decided to disconnect your "wanter." The wants we have can be complicated, difficult to attain, and often too expensive for our current budget. Wanting can be time consuming, exhausting and overwhelming. Can you see why you might want to tone down, or disconnect it?

When you came into the world, you wanted to be fed, warm, and dry. As you got older, you wanted more food, toys to play with, and friends to be with you when you played with your toys. The more you wanted, the more consequences you had around wanting. At first, your parents were very solicitous about giving you whatever you wanted, but as you grew older, they said "no" more often. They might have even raised their voice or humiliated you in public when they said no. You learned that you couldn't always have what you wanted, and then you learned that even asking for something might get you time in your bedroom or a swat on the rear. You eventually learned to be circumspect about your wanting, only asking for things that you really wanted, and in a way that wouldn't result in Mom and Dad grabbing your hand and un-ceremonially marching you out of the store.

Then you left home to live on your own, and you began to realize why your parents said no so often. Wanting things was expensive, not to mention disappointing, humiliating, and downright painful when you failed to get what you wanted. You've had millions of experiences of wanting and the consequences of not getting. Consequently, you have very deep neuro-pathways of engrained beliefs resulting from your wanting—and not getting—experiences. Remember, our beliefs are created by what we think and our beliefs create feelings and behavior.

You've experienced huge displeasure around wanting. There was that house you wanted which you purchased at the top of the market and lost to foreclosure four years later. There was that boyfriend you wanted to marry, and did ten years ago. Now he is fighting you for full custody of your children in the divorce. There was the best friend who you were so excited to go on vacation to Hawaii with, but she left you alone in the condo night after night while she took up with the lifeguard she met on the beach. There was that business partner who convinced you to invest your hard earned cash as the down payment for the condo project, and then left town with the proceeds from the construction loan.

Another reason your "wanter" is broken is because society is continually training you to accept a cultural version of success. You think you want the four-bedroom house in the Hamptons because your brother says that is the best place to live. He is your older brother and you have always wanted to be just like him. You accept the hype you read and hear from the media about how only the rich and famous are good enough to live in the Hamptons. You want to be rich and famous and good enough, so you work your tail off to make the money to buy the place your brother picks out for you. Within three years, you have gained fifty pounds, have high blood pressure, and are now getting a divorce. You don't realize that the decline in your health and relationship is the result of the stress and unhappiness you feel driving in heavy traffic to work every day. You really want to live in a simple apartment and walk to work, but you are confused by all the messages you get that you should want a bigger life. The life that may be right for your brother but is definitely not right for you!

It takes a huge amount of courage to disconnect from the influence that our society has on us. It takes personal power and strength to define our own definition of success. If you don't get off the treadmill trying to keep up with the Joneses, you'll never find your way to your own success and happiness. By the way, the success you see on commercials, and in television and the movies, isn't necessarily real success. Television is the main communicator of the belief viruses that keep us stuck. We know real life isn't like the movies, but we often don't want to admit it. We can easily be taken in by the beautiful world that is depicted on the silver screen. We can be convinced that we will never be happy unless we live in that perfectly manicured house, wearing designer clothes, eating an incredible meal on a dining table designed by Martha Stewart. The advertising industry born in the *Mad Men* era has a huge impact on our "wanter." It is confusing to figure out whether what we want comes from our inner self or from a desire installed by some powerful image we saw in the media.

Yes, you can create the life of your dreams, but there is a fine line between a realistic dream and fantasy. The dream machine can dream up anything, so it is up to us to determine the difference. Going after a fantasy life can lead to disappointment. When we are continually disappointed, we disconnect our "wanter." When that isn't functioning, reinvention can't happen. Your happiness will come from creating your own version of success. That is why we call it an "authentic life" because it is *your* life, one that you design to perfectly match who you are and what experiences and possessions really ring your chimes.

I'M NEVER GOING TO DO THAT AGAIN

Have you ever heard yourself say out loud, "I'm never going to do *that* again?" We all say it from time to time, especially when we are feeling strong emotions and reacting to something that didn't work out. What you mean when you say you are never going to get married again is that you are never going to let yourself *want* to get married again. When you disconnect your "wanter" in one area of your life, you disconnect it in every area of your life. Your "wanter" can't spring into action so you can get a better job, but stay quiet when you run into a handsome man at Starbucks.

We trick ourselves into believing our "wanter" is still in working condition by allowing ourselves to want something that is easy to get. Women who say they will never get married again tell me they want to date. What happens if they run into the man of their dreams on a date? It seems like emotional whiplash to me when you say, "Yes, let's get to know each other, but if you want to get close, no way because I'm never going to do *that* again." Think about it. Your "wanter" is either on or it's off, and if you want a better life, you have to do what it takes to keep it on.

Many of you have turned your "wanter" off to keep yourself safe and I understand why. You have many fears as a result of wanting and not getting. It feels very scary to even consider turning on the dream machine and letting your imagination fill your head with pictures of what you really want but may never be able to get. I ask you: Are you happy now, diligently squashing your wanting every time you feel its pull? I suggest you probably aren't. Perhaps the path to a happy life is the pursuit of what you want based on your authentic inner urgings, the pursuit of contributing your verse to the world's song. Would it be worth it to turn your "wanter" on again, full force, if it meant that you could connect to the passion and purpose you have always hoped to connect with? Would it be worth it to want freely if it meant that was the only way you would ever experience exquisite joy? Perhaps you haven't gotten what you really wanted before in your life because you didn't know the specific action steps to take to get it. If you follow The Reinvention Blueprint,™ you will learn proven manifesting skills that will ensure your dreams will become a reality.

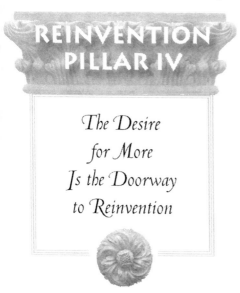

REINVENTION
PILLAR IV

*The Desire
for More
Is the Doorway
to Reinvention*

Turning your "wanter" back on could be a big decision for you. I know its rusty, and it will take a little time to polish it up and get it working on high again, but I invite you to consider right now if this is what you are willing to do. The first step to waking up your "wanter" is to begin to get to know yourself better. Take it one step at a time, and turn your attention to your preferences. It can be simple at first. Food, clothes, and leisure activities are all fertile ground for you to practice learning what you really want. In fact, I see these areas as a harmless playground for exploring my preferences and desires and getting my "wanter" in shape. I recently decided to explore wearing only white. The same fears come up—what will people think, what will they say? It is so powerful to exercise your independence and to do what you want, and allowing everyone to have their own reaction. Reinvention depends on having a healthy "wanter" and practicing on a regular basis is necessary. Once your have a few positive experiences, you will get back on track and soon your dream machine will create thrilling new possibilities for your consideration.

WHAT DO I WANT RIGHT NOW?

Once you graduate from "wanter" rehab, you can consider seriously reinventing your life. Ask yourself the question, "What do I want right now?" several times a day. Make it a new habit and ask it every day for the rest of your life. The more you ask the question, the more your "wanter" will do its job. This is very good news, don't you think? You make a choice and already you have new beliefs to support your reinvention!

In Nichiren Buddhism, there is a concept that teaches us that the pursuit of our earthly desires contributes to enlightenment. Enlightenment means different things to different people. I describe enlightenment as gaining a deeper and deeper understanding of our spiritual self as we live our human life. I also believe there are stages of enlightenment and that we don't have to wait to celebrate our enlightenment until some future indefinable end. We get to acknowledge and celebrate each new awareness and level of understanding along the way. Celebration is a very important part of reinvention. When your "wanter" is doing its job, celebrate everything you get. Celebrating the milestones along your journey will ensure that your "wanter" will stay happy and healthy forever.

As we pursue our desires, we gain wisdom about ourselves and about the mystery of life in the process. Running a marathon may fill us with a sense of accomplishment, but soon that feeling fades, and we have to choose another mountain to climb. What is truly valuable is the journey along the way to running the marathon. When we face our fears and overcome our desire to give up, we learn lessons that never leave us. In the pursuit of getting what we want in life, we receive both the satisfaction of accomplishing our goals, as well as the inner growth that we need to keep moving forward toward achieving higher desires. Everything we do in life has the potential to teach us something important about ourselves that can be used along the journey to enlightenment and authentic, joyful living.

A REMINDER ABOUT WANTING

Pausing to ask yourself just exactly what you want, not what you think you "should" want, what others want you to want, or what others want for you, can often be a surprisingly emotional exercise. It can be deeply moving if you have denied yourself for a long time by disengaging your "wanter." Allowing it to come back online may require real courage, especially if you haven't processed old pain and experiences from your past that caused you to turn it off in the first place. An exercise in The Reinvention Blueprint™ called *Creating a Reinvention Life Vision* is designed to help you uncover old baggage and remove it so your "wanter" can return to functioning at full power.

MANDY'S WANTS

Mandy found this to be true as she learned more about reinventing her life. Her childhood was chaotic, her father was an abusive alcoholic, and her mother struggled to keep the family together. After recovering from heart surgery, Mandy had the "if not now, when" epiphany. She was growing older and she was finally ready to put her life ahead of everyone else's. As she began considering the different areas of life and how she wanted to improve things, she experienced limiting beliefs and strong emotional reactions. "Little voices would creep in telling me 'You're not good enough' or 'Who do you think you are to want that?' These voices would make me doubt myself and I would question whether I deserved to have a better life," she explained.

Together, Mandy and I used several techniques, including Byron Katie's "The Work" and Dr. Deborah Sandella's RIM Method, a powerful technique to dissolve limiting beliefs in which I am certified to practice. Through these methods, Mandy was able to let go of a significant amount of pain, anger, and trauma left over from incidents in her past. She credits this inner work as the main reason she feels free and confident to reinvent her life.

Mandy used her desire to overcome her doubts as motivation to begin a daily practice of meditation, prayer, visualization, and gratitude. She says a gratitude prayer every morning and makes a list of every success she achieves. "I literally have written down a lot of the things that I have learned and achieved over the past few years so when I have doubt or my self-talk is negative, I can get the list out and remind myself how far I've come," she said. "I've looked at it so often over the years it's all tattered and frayed around the edges. My list is invaluable when I sink down into the depths and need to remember how far I've come."

Her list includes achieving her goal to create a closer relationship with her grown children and grandchildren. When we met, she told me about the tension that existed in those relationships because they had never discussed some of the things that happened during their childhood. Over the past two years, Mandy has quietly and gracefully brought up some of the incidents and helped her children process their feelings so they could let them go. Mandy is always headed to some event at the school or over to her children's homes to be involved with family activities. "They are the light of my life," she reports, "I am forever grateful that I now have skills to have the relationship with my kids that I never had with my parents."

Mandy's big dream is to teach teens *The Passion Test*. A few years ago, she made a goal to study with Janet and Chris Attwood, authors of *The Passion Test: The Effortless Path to Discovering Your Destiny*. She has attended several workshops with them and in the summer of 2013, she traveled to India with Janet Atwood and several other teachers, assisting in local *Passion Test* workshops and visiting several ashrams. "By working with *The Passion Test*, I realized that my passion was to teach kids how to find their passions! I hope to make a real difference through this work. I visualize doing workshops in schools, working one on one with kids, and empowering parents to set a good example for their kids by following their own passions. I want to do my part to heal the world."

WALKING THROUGH THE DOOR

In order to reinvent your life into what you really want to do, be, or have, you will have to face the fire of what made you turn your "wanter" off in the first place. If you are clear that you want to have a different life, then facing your past is a "do it now or do it later" proposition. As long as you cling to the belief that pushing away your fears and pain will protect you, your life will remain in its current discontented state. It is only when you acknowledge what happened, and process the pain so you can let it go, that you will be released to reinvent your life. You are made to do this. You will feel the pain *and* you will survive it. We all do. It only takes a moment for you to square your shoulders and say "yes." Say yes to living the life of your dreams. Say yes to embracing the power you were born with. Say yes to healing Her and yes to reinventing Her.

Walk through the door to your own transformation. Look at each area of your life and identify the door you want to walk through. Is it the door of reinventing your relationships? Is it the door of leaving the job that sucks out your soul every day so you can buy the bakery shop on the corner? Is it the door of being the first person in your family to graduate from college? Many of us don't let ourselves have what we want because we are afraid if we do, our spouse, friends, or family might not like the change. We are afraid of conflict, of possibly losing the relationship. It's true, if you change yourself, your relationships will change. If you are reinventing—transforming—you can always invite your family and friends to change along with you, to create new and better relationships. When I did my first personal growth training in 1998, my sister and I did it together. Over the next few years, other members of our family also took part. It is one of the most rewarding aspects of our family togetherness; we are committed to healing ourselves and reinventing our lives together.

If it isn't time for your spouse or best friend to reinvent his/her life, then accept the inevitability that is the path of your life. You might not understand why things happen in your life at first, but over time you will see that everything in your life happens for a reason—a *good* reason. Relationships ebb and flow. They change every day. Someone comes into your life, stays for a while, and then moves on. Reinvention provides an opportunity to trust the wisdom of how your life evolves without needing to always control it.

Reinventing You

Pillar IV reminds us that what we desire is absolutely essential for our reinvention. Pick one area of your life that you want to reinvent and invite your "wanter" to engage.

Ask yourself over and over "What do I want?" and write down your answers. Then, put your dream machine into action and imagine having everything you desire. Do your best to free your "wanter" to speak in her empowered voice. If you feel silly at first, just keep going. Your "wanter" will enjoy the work out, so have fun!

Chapter Five

Divorce Your Money
Reinvent Your Life

CHAPTER FIVE
DIVORCE YOUR MONEY—
REINVENT YOUR LIFE

YOUR RELATIONSHIP WITH MONEY

*I*n order to reinvent your financial life, and therefore achieve better results, it's important to explore your personal relationship with money. Money is funny. Not in a "ha ha" way, but in a "Isn't it weird what people think and feel about money?" way. I told a friend of mine the other day that after years of observing the weird way people are with money, it's almost like they consider money as another body part. Some people hold it close as if it were another arm. Other people reject it as if it were pockets of cellulite on their thighs. Our beliefs about money are so confusing that we often act like it is a problem. We definitely want more of it, yet when we get it, we treat it like an ugly stepchild. We ignore it, abuse it, and get mad at it for making us do things we don't want to do. It's no wonder we are confused about money.

Our society has made having money, and getting more of it, the main focus of our lives. We gauge our own worth as a human being based on how much money we do or don't have. We spend kilowatts of energy, and money, proving to our friends and neighbors that we have as much, and probably more, than they have. If we can prove that we have more money, then people will think of us as special. We spend a lot of energy trying to be special. The woman with a three-bedroom home is assumed to have more money than the woman with the two-bedroom home. If she drives a Porsche, she is assumed to have more money than the woman who drives a Toyota. Of course, our assumptions might be totally wrong, but we cling to the meaning of the measurements because doing so makes us feel better about ourselves.

The only problem with the measurements is that it's easy to lie about how much money we have. I might drive a Porsche, but it might be leased and I live in a studio apartment on the poor side of town. I might live in a five-bedroom home, but I haven't paid my mortgage payment for over a year and you wouldn't even know it.

The purpose of money is that it is there to support what is important and meaningful in our lives, and in order to reinvent our life it will require us to have a healthy and productive relationship with money. It's as simple as that.

MONEY IS A TOOL

Money is a tool, nothing else—a tool to help you create and reinvent the life of your dreams. An easy way to understand this is to think about the collection of tools you have in the garage. Think about the hammer collection in your garage. You wouldn't lock them up, or never let anyone see them, only to use a different tool to do a hammer's job, would you? That is what we call hoarding or scarcity. You wouldn't go out and buy a bunch of hammers and then give them all away to your friends so you don't have one when you need it, would you? You might call that giving or selfless, but I call it unworthy behavior. In order to experience a healthy and productive relationship with money, you must separate it from your self-image, your self-confidence, and your self-esteem.

You use your hammer when you need it, and then you put it down and don't think about it until you need it again. What if you were to think about your money in the same way? Yes, I get that money is more complicated than a hammer, but when you put it in its proper place in your mind, and make proper choices about how to use it, you have everything you need to build your reinvention. Wouldn't it be a relief to know that money is just another tool you have at your disposal? Look at it another way. You don't obsess, lose sleep, or fight with your spouse about the hammer, do you? Why would you do so about your money? Let me repeat myself. Money is just a tool.

Many of us need a makeover when it comes to how we think and feel about money. I like to think about money as if it were a river—a river flowing right in front of me. I dip my hand into the flow and take a little out when I need it. The river continues to flow no matter what is happening around me. Sometimes the flow is heavier and sometimes it's lighter, but it continues to flow. I encourage you to consider viewing your money in the same way. Doing so would be more helpful than continually obsessing over whether you will have enough and convincing yourself that you probably don't. If you believe money will continue to flow, then it will! If you believe it won't, then it most likely won't.

Yes, money is a tool and it is also a flow. There really are those aspects to it. You get to choose how you dip in, how much you take out, and for what purpose. Money can be simple or it can be hard. Money becomes hard when we identify ourselves with it, when we obsess about it, when we crave it, or when we link our happiness to it. When we see our value as a person connected to how much money we do or don't have, we make bad choices—sometimes foolish choices. Think of the people who jumped off buildings because they lost money in the Great Depression. In fact, people are still jumping off buildings because of their issues with money. Why would someone take their own life unless they felt like they couldn't be happy without money or didn't deserve to live without money? Why would anyone destroy himself or herself just because they lost a tool? I don't mean to disturb you, but an extreme example such as this might help you realize how important it is for you to divorce money so you can reinvent your life. If you internalize your money in any way, then divorce your money right now!

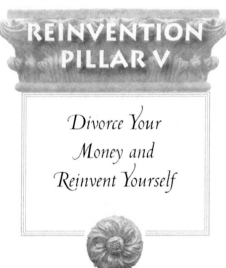

REINVENTION PILLAR V

Divorce Your Money and Reinvent Yourself

Separate yourself from the view that you, or your behavior with money, in any way, reflects who you are, how important your life is, or how much value you have to another person, place, or thing. Look around at your life and identify the people in it who are successfully seeing and using money as a tool to reinvent their life. I think Donald Trump is a good example of someone who uses money as a tool. You might not like his personality, but I think it's obvious that Donald uses money, along with his other talents and interests, to reinvent his life—and he sure seems to be having fun doing it! Another man, brilliant at using money as a tool for creating an incredible life, as well as to serve humanity, was Steve Jobs. We can't forget Bill Gates, Warren Buffett, and Jeff Bezos, to name only a few of the living icons who also are making a huge difference with their money and having a ball doing it!

What about the women? At the top of the list would be Oprah, of course. She is a great example of a woman who started with nothing and learned to reinvent herself to make a huge difference educating and empowering women around the globe. Oprah's success is a study in trusting and believing in oneself, as well as co-creating her life with a Higher Power. Other women to thank for their example as stars of financial reinvention are Hillary Clinton, Beyoncé Knowles, Arianna Huffington, and J.K. Rowling, to name a few of my favorites.

There are so many examples of men and women who have proved that money can expand, not limit our lives. The only difference between them and you is their relationship with money. Well, there are more differences of course, but you can't argue that you started on a level playing field with most superstars. Perhaps they had different messages about money growing up and different opportunities, but they are human beings just like you and me. No matter what money messages you were born with, no matter how much you think you have messed up your money in the past, you have the same gifts inside as the people you admire in order to help you create whatever you want financially. You have the power to see money as a tool, an easy-to-use tool that human beings designed as a means to pay for the goods and services we need for our life. It was not designed to become the focus of our life, nor as something that we measure our value as a human being. Period.

Take that in for a moment. Money was not invented as a measurement of your value as a human being. Yet, you behave as if it was. It's our culture that has convinced you of this and you have chosen to take on this belief as your own. You can just as eas-

> ## YOU CAN ONLY GO FORWARD BY MAKING MISTAKES

ily choose another belief, one that works better for your life and what you are about. If you have a belief that the amount of money you do or don't have defines you, you can choose to let it go right now. You can create a new belief that money is a tool and a flow, and it is always available for you to pick up and apply to the reinvention of your life whenever you want to. The flow is always available to you, and you are the one who determines the size of the flow and how and when you dip into it. Money doesn't control you, so stop letting it! You control money, so start making choices that provide you with what you want to create in your life. It's a tool, it's a tool, it's a tool... and the more you treat it as a tool, the more it will flow into your life.

STOPPING THE FLOW

There is an unfortunate habit that many women have developed around money that can stop the flow. We make mistakes with money and then feel guilty about it. We overdraw our checking account, charge groceries on our credit card, and under contribute to our retirement account. Almost every day we see an article on the Internet or hear a story on the news about the "proper" way to manage money. We compare our money management with the article we read in Money Magazine and decide we come up short. We continually judge ourselves harshly for our perceived mistakes with money. We carry overwhelming feelings of guilt and shame over credit card debt, losing a house to foreclosure, or the fact we filed for bankruptcy ten years ago. We have a habit of feeling bad about ourselves, and believing that we are bad for making those mistakes just reinforces the bad feeling.

It's not going to help your reinvention to continue thinking this way. We know that making mistakes is how we learn. This is what we teach our children. But when it comes to money, it seems like there is so much more at stake. We believe that making mistakes with money is really bad and then we take the leap to believing we are bad.

I hear this one in almost every conversation I have with a woman about her money. She is completely convinced that she is a bad money manager and that there is no hope for her in the future. If you feel this way too, I have to warn you that until you change your mind, change your belief, you will have trouble trusting yourself to make good decisions in the future. Once you stop trusting yourself, you stop believing that money is a flow. When you stop believing that money is a flow, then that is what you will experience—money will no longer flow. It's a self-fulfilling decline of one mistake leading to another and embracing your beliefs that you are bad with money and bad all over. You are not bad no matter how many mistakes you made with money.

THE BELIEF VIRUS OF SCARCITY

You wouldn't take your mistakes with money so seriously if you didn't suffer from a scarcity mentality. Don't fret. You are definitely not alone on this one. A search on Amazon.com under the word "scarcity" brought up 1,500 book titles. Scarcity thinking is just that—thinking. There is new research that indicates that scarcity thinking is born from emotional deprivation in childhood. Emotional deprivation can lead to feelings of insecurity that contribute to an overall feeling that we lack in some department. We feel that we don't have enough food, enough love, enough money, or enough time. Scarcity thinking creates anxiety that is the precursor to being vulnerable to temptation. Our anxiety can lead to the roller coaster of over-eating and then crash dieting, of over-spending and then hoarding.

Scarcity behavior comes from a series of thoughts and beliefs, and just like all the other beliefs that I've been pointing out to you, the good news is that you don't have to continue to live in the shadow of the past. You can change your beliefs and you can change your financial results. All it takes is the choice to get started on processing and shredding your past one step at a time.

Natural Law of Attraction

If scarcity thinking contributes to our lack of money, then how can we turn things around? Under the law of attraction, the theory is that if you believe that there isn't enough money, enough food, or enough love in your life, then that is what you will experience. By contrast, if you believe that there is more than enough for you and for everyone around you, then that is what you will experience. The belief that there is more than enough to go around is what we call abundance thinking. A finer point about the law of attraction, and believing that abundance is all around you, is that it requires you be willing to accept the truth

of it without being able to prove it. This is another time when "believing is seeing" comes into play. When you believe that you live in an abundant universe, even if you can't always see it, only then will you experience it. Once you believe it, you will achieve it.

The reality of your current situation with money, whether it's scarcity or abundance, is entirely based on how you think about it. Remember, we think our world into existence. Once you choose to get your thinking aligned with what you want to create in your life, then you will easily manifest it into being. This might be something you want to underline because it's important for you to remember during your reinvention. I suggest you study the law of attraction. In a search on Amazon.com under "law of attraction," 2,600 titles came up. Take your pick. I recommend *Money and the Law of Attraction: Learning to Attract Wealth, Health, and Happiness* by Esther and Jerry Hicks.

If you are emotionally conflicted about money because of something in your past, you will have challenges making good choices with money in the future. If any so-called "shameful" incidents have happened to you, such as credit card debt or foreclosure, and you still feel bad about it, I encourage you to take action in whatever way works for you in order to heal your pain and forgive yourself. Internalizing past emotions around money will hold you back from the glorious reinvention you just dreamed of in the previous chapter. I wouldn't want that to happen to you.

> *You will not be able to solve anything outside until you own how the situation affects you inside...*
>
> —MICHAEL SINGER
> *The Untethered Soul:*
> *The Journey Beyond Yourself*

According to Dr. Brad Klontz and Dr. Ted Klontz, co-authors of *Mind Over Money: Overcoming the Money Disorders That Threaten our Financial Health*, many of us have early childhood events, called financial flashpoints, that leave such an impression on us that they still impact our behavior as adults. "From childhood interpretations of financial flashpoint events, we develop a set of beliefs about money called *money scripts*. The more profound the original event, the more strongly our emotions lock the money script in place," they said.

They go on to explain that it is natural for us to make judgments about what happens to us in life, but it's when we cling to those beliefs, and don't question how they make us behave, that it can become problematic. To free ourselves from old money scripts that no longer work for us, we must first deal with any unfinished business left over from the original event. Once we do that step, we can learn new ways to think about and deal with money. Here again, "The Work" and the RIM Method are good tools for tackling those early childhood memories.

Your history with money is just that—your history. You cannot change it, but you can embrace it as a learning experience and make a new choice for today and tomorrow. Feeling bad about money is not necessary. It won't make other people think more highly of you, and it won't change what has gone before. You can't reinvent your life from negative feelings. Keeping it present by continually feeling bad about it just embeds it deeper into your brain and makes it harder to let go. Learn from it, yes; process the pain about it, yes; but, in the end, just let it go. Let it go and turn toward your future. That is where new thinking about money can truly improve your life.

In my past, I used credit cards to buy clothes, food, alcohol, and travel to make myself feel better. I wasn't aware of the deep hole of need that I had inside and that I was driven by a subconscious belief that buying new things would make me feel better. It did, for a while, but I had to keep upping the ante to achieve the same goal. You know the rest of the story. It was only through admitting that there was a connection between the way I work on the inside, to what was happening on the outside, that I was able to shift the tide and reinvent my life.

Unfortunately, most of us have a love/hate relationship with money. We crave it and we despise it, all at the same time.

How can we expect to have success with something that we have such strong and conflicting emotions about? If you felt the same feelings about your partner, you would be sitting in the therapist's office in a flash. At least I hope you would be. Yet, many of us hesitate to do anything to heal our dysfunctional relationship with money. We don't even question how we are with money most of the time.

How do you divorce money? How do you change your unhealthy relationship to a healthy and productive one? Stop internalizing and projecting that who you are is based on money, and put it in its proper place in your life. Money is a tool at your disposal to pick up or put down in order to reinvent your life.

RICH VS. WEALTHY

Recently, I was honored to speak to a group of medical residents about starting off on the right foot with money. They are poised, as you may be as you reinvent your life, on the precipice of managing more money than they have been used to. I spoke of the incredible pressure that our culture puts on us to become rich. There is a cultural belief that doctors make a lot of money, so doctors feel the pressure to reflect that in their lifestyle. The reality is that most doctors make a good living, but not a great living. This will become even truer as our healthcare system changes, both in the way doctors charge for their services and how patients and insurance companies pay them. Most new doctors today have the largest amounts of student loan debt in history. I urged the residents to create a healthy relationship with money from the beginning, so they will be able to meet both their obligations and their desire for an abundant lifestyle.

I explained to them there is a difference between becoming rich and growing wealth. It may sound exciting to win the lottery, or hit a big jackpot in Las Vegas, or even to be left an inheritance. Easy money is always attractive. There have been many studies on how people behave when they receive easy money. Over 50% of lottery winners spend all of their winnings within five years. You might think that you wouldn't do the same thing, but the truth is that people have a belief about how much money they should have, or can handle. We call it our financial "set point." When people receive an amount significantly higher than their financial set point, they freak out. Their subconscious belief systems spring into action and they sabotage their good fortune. They get rid of it because they didn't earn it. They can't hold on to it because it isn't theirs. They are out of their comfort zone, have hit their upper limit, and spending the money gets them back to where they feel safe, inside their set point and their comfort zone.

I read a story about one lottery winner who was being sued by several family members, was addicted to drugs and alcohol, and was robbed of large amounts of cash several times. He also lost several million dollars buying options in the stock market. This all happened to one man who was obviously way out of his comfort zone with his new circumstances. His ego was so frightened by the responsibility of managing such a large amount of money that it did everything it could to get him to get rid of the money so he could go back into his comfort zone! The most incredible part of the story is that this man was already a millionaire when he won the lottery! Our beliefs about money are powerful and if we are unconscious about how they drive our behavior, we could end up back where we started.

Easy money and becoming rich can be seductive, but real wealth is something you build every single day with every single choice you make. Wealth requires a healthy relationship with money and the willingness to be conscious about your beliefs and early messages about money. You have to systematically change the beliefs that no longer support your dreams. There are times when you might take big leaps ahead in your wealth, but wealth is accumulated through years of earning income and making choices about how to save it, spend it, and invest it. If you decide from the beginning that you are going to be the pilot of smart financial decisions, and be patient and steadfast on your quest for wealth, you will be more likely to achieve it. Being rich can be fleeting. Achieving wealth is forever.

DO WHAT YOU LOVE AND THE MONEY WILL FOLLOW

In order to become wealthy in money, you must become wealthy in spirit. That is the difference between rich and wealthy. The rich often show little or no spirit (which is why we don't like many rich people), and the wealthy almost always do. In order to achieve wealth, you will need to grow yourself and your life to be ready to receive it. In order to become wealthy, you will need to learn how to use money as your tool and be in the right state of mind about the journey. That's why most people never attain wealth. They don't believe they deserve it, don't believe they are worthy of it, and they aren't willing to grow themselves into the person they need to be in order to receive it. But you aren't "most" people. You are unique and powerful and ready to reinvent your life and your relationship with money. You know what you need to do now and you are ready to take it on.

You have a role to play, a purpose to embody, and a passion to give to others. You were put on this earth, at this moment in time, to expand into your true self. You stand for something and you are a person who other people want to follow and emulate. You choose to let go of your mask, to speak your truth, and to become everything you were meant to be. You see your potential, and you see the door, and nothing will stop you from walking through it. You are ready to sculpt yourself into your own version of Venus (the goddess of femininity) and you are ready to live in abundance. You are ready to chip away everything that is not as beautiful and powerful as you know you are designed to be. You are ready to Reinvent Her.

Reinventing You

Pillar V calls on you to divorce your relationship with money so that you are free to reinvent yourself, but to do that, we have to look at what's working. An example of what is working could be that you and your partner have an easy time talking about and making joint financial decisions.

On the flip side, consider your relationship with money and what parts of it you want to divorce. What isn't working in your life with money? An example of something that might not be working could be your tendency to eat out too much, which causes you to live paycheck to paycheck.

After you list three or four elements of your relationship with money that you would like to divorce, write down how doing so would free you to reinvent your life. If you were more conscious about how much you are actually spending on dining out, what would change in your life? Take this opportunity to raise your awareness about the financial area, so you can begin to reinvent and change your results. This exercise promises to pay huge and immediate dividends in your life!

Chapter Six

The Reinvention
Blueprint™

CHAPTER SIX
THE REINVENTION BLUEPRINT™

REINVENTING HER:
HELPING WOMEN PLAN, PURSUE, AND
CAPITALIZE ON THEIR NEXT CHAPTER

*T*his idea, concept, program, book, and movement has been growing within me since 2008. Early that year, my life had taken another interesting turn, in that the Universe served me yet another huge life lesson. I opened my financial planning practice in 2003 and threw everything into it during the first three years. Telling you all the ups and downs of starting a business from scratch could fill another, much less interesting book, so I won't give you all the boring details here. Just know that the learning curve was steep, and I was pretty much burned out by the fall of 2006. Searching for a solution to an unsustainable situation, I decided to seek a partner for my company in order to add more bandwidth for my clients, as well as reduce my level of stress. It seemed as if the perfect option showed up easily, but looking back it was obvious I was in a hurry and rushed into the decision. I did a cursory job of investigation, and ultimately picked a partner who was a poor match for my clients, my reinvention, and me. I was blind to my mistake until those sticks, 2x4s, and eventually another house, dropped on my head again.

The reinvention journey provides opportunities at every turn for us to learn more about ourselves and refine our purpose in life. I focused my attention so completely on surviving the first few years of a new business that I forgot, denied, or literally ignored practically everything I had learned during my reinvention in my forties. There were many signs that I had made a mistake in merging my company with another, yet I chose to ignore them and lie to myself—choosing to believe that nothing was wrong. I was just going through an adjustment. The project never worked because I had different values than my new partner, as well as different beliefs about the role a financial advisor should play in a client's life. I never fit in with the staff or the culture, but I was unwilling to admit the possibility that my decision might have been misguided. The house dropped on me one day in the form of complete and total rejection of what I stood for and the contribution I believed I was making, by my partner and his staff. It was devastating. So I did what every self-defeated woman would do when rejected completely by her peers and co-workers. I went home and cried for two days. Really.

Divine intervention saved me again. The tear in my relationship with my partner and staff was irreparable. I picked myself up, brushed myself off, and took steps to end our partnership so I could become an independent company once again. I was terrified that I wouldn't be able to maintain the energy level required to provide all that my loyal clients needed and deserved. One of the difficult elements of reinvention, and living life in general, is that we only get to see ahead as far as the next curve on our journey. To succeed in life, and reinvention, we have to learn to trust—trust in the process and trust in ourselves. I didn't know how I would reinvent my business this time, but I had to trust that divine guidance would show me the way. It did, and in a way I could never have guessed.

It presented me an opportunity to attend the Sun Valley Wellness Festival, an annual event in Sun Valley Idaho where top speakers and practitioners of mind, body, and spirit present on topics focused on improving overall wellness. I was guided to attend a workshop held the day before the annual Memorial Day weekend event. My sister and I were excited to hear Muriel Hemingway speak about her new book on yoga and healthy living. The person who was to introduce Muriel apologized that she wouldn't be speaking that day due to a recent illness. The introducer also reassured us that our ticket would not go to waste as Muriel had asked a close friend who was in town to fill in for her. Skeptical that anyone could take the place of Muriel, we went into shock when Anthony Robbins, the father of the life coaching industry, and his wife Sage walked into the room.

This was an extraordinary and synchronistic event for this man to be with this group of people that afternoon. Tony and Sage proceeded to wow us for two hours with stories of their search for a cure for Sage's debilitating motion sickness. The cure turned out to be a spiritual transfer of divine grace known as "Oneness Blessing." On the Oneness website, www.onenessuniversity.org, the founders of the movement describe Oneness as "an inner transformation and awakening into higher states of consciousness. Deeksha, or Oneness Blessing, is a process by which divine grace initiates a journey into higher states of consciousness. The Deeksha is believed to affect different lobes of the physical brain, thereby reducing stress levels and intensifying the levels of love, joy, and awareness. Millions across the globe testify about the calming and awakening effects of the Oneness Deeksha, which is slowly gaining recognition as by far the easiest and most effective approach to enriching human consciousness."

The Robbins' synchronistic journey from frustration and discouragement to restoring Sage's health was nothing short of awe inspiring. Their gift to us at the end of our time together was to join other Blessing Givers and lay their hands on our heads so we could all experience Oneness Blessings. I felt myself floating above the floor and experienced one of the peak spiritual experiences of my life. When someone describes a personal experience that they consider a major life break-through, it can be hard to believe if it didn't happen to you. That afternoon, I experienced a divine interruption in my life—a dividing line between the confused and fearful state of mind that I walked into the room with, and the confident and inspired state of mind I walked out with. I was touched to my core, and mysterious as it was, I left with complete confidence that there would be a new direction for my life and that I would embrace it easily.

Tony and Sage were indeed the highlight of the weekend, but I was equally excited to hear Dan Millman, author of *The Way of the Peaceful Warrior*. I read his book and watched the movie several times, and Dan's encouragement to trust our higher consciousness to guide us on our path to wellness resonated in my heart. It seemed to me that every speaker I heard that weekend was there to provide me with just the right message and reassurance that I had everything I needed, right inside me, to successfully and joyfully navigate the next phase of my reinvention. All I needed was to connect with my spirit again and apply the same skills and awareness that I knew were there and available to me. I was sent there to remember who I really was, and to walk through another door to freedom.

I have attended Wellness Festivals every year since 2008 and have been inspired and motivated by Jill Bolte Taylor, Greg Braden, Robert Kennedy, and last year's keynote speaker Dr. Eben Alexander, author of *Proof of Heaven: A Neurosurgeons Journey Into the Afterlife.* In 2010, I declared my intention to be chosen as a speaker on the topic of our inner dynamic and wellness with money. In 2013, my dream came true and in 2014, I will return for my second year as a speaker and to launch this book. If you are looking for a unique experience of learning from top thought leaders on mind, body, and spirit wholeness, I recommend you attend the Sun Valley Wellness Festival. It is indeed a unique and powerful opportunity to supplement your reinvention resources.

After my Oneness Blessing and life changing experience at the 2008 Wellness Festival, I returned home newly empowered to re-establish my business with confidence and clarity. I realized that the axiom "what doesn't break you makes you stronger" was true for me in this period of my reinvention. I had survived a series of tough life lessons, and I was stronger for it. Have you ever heard the saying "everything happens for a reason?" I have experienced that to be true many times as I reflect back on my life. I am lucky enough to have lived almost six decades now, so I can also tell you with confidence that each experience is linked to the next and to the next. It seems that we experience a chain of events that happen for a reason and once you understand and surrender to their unfolding, your life becomes both exciting and peaceful at the same time. I didn't realize it then, but the lessons I learned from the misfortune of my partnership actually prepared me for a bigger challenge yet to come. It was the fall of 2008, and my reinvention would include a period where I would need all of my inner strength and talents to assist my clients through the trauma of the economic collapse.

Surviving the Great Recession and resulting real estate, stock market, and employment crash provided more fuel to stoke the fire of new passion in me. The events of the past five years have changed every single one of us. The collapse of the housing market, high unemployment, and the realization that our financial security can be lost seemingly overnight, has created new fears and emotional trauma for a lot of people. Many of you may not have fully recovered yet, you may have lost your home to foreclosure, have a job that is below your abilities and income needs, and had to liquidate your retirement plan to pay the bills. You have experienced pain and fear at a level that you were most likely unprepared for. If you are like most people, you haven't truly acknowledged how deeply the events may have impacted your ability to trust the financial system, our government, or even yourself. If you haven't explored your inner feelings about what happened to you personally, you will struggle with reinventing your life. Just like the events of the past that have caused hurt and limiting beliefs, this event needs to be processed and let go of in the same way so you can be free to create whatever is next for you.

Watching how deeply our predicament impacted my clients, friends, and family, and how their beliefs caused them to react in ways that weren't helpful, I knew it was time to move. It was time to shine the light on the real reasons that our country made such drastic mistakes. It was time to help people understand the connection between their thoughts, beliefs, and emotions and the results they realize in their lives. We don't always connect these dots because most of us were never taught how. Our lack of understanding about our inner dynamic is especially disconcerting when it comes to managing money and building financial security, but it also applies to our lack of success at work, our poor health, and the dysfunction in our relationships. If we don't see how our inner dynamic impacts how we live our lives, then we can quite unknowingly sabotage the very happiness and freedom that we are all striving for.

MY ANSWER TO SOLVING OUR PROBLEMS

I designed a "personal development guide"—a step-by-step process, for women in particular, to follow as they seek a more rewarding life. I wanted to help people who were ready to navigate the tricky process of changing their lives for the better. Most of us don't like the word "change," because we believe change is scary and difficult. Remember that our thoughts create our reality, so if you want to alter your belief about change, I wholeheartedly invite you to do so. You could alter your belief from "change is scary and difficult," to "change is easy and I am on my way to living the life of my dreams!" I like that belief so much better than the "change is scary" one, don't you?

Why are we so afraid of change? The simple reason is that our ego is fiercely committed to keeping us safe, and so are our family, friends, and co-workers. If we try to change or improve our lives, everyone around us puts up a fight. The people in our life don't want us to change because it might require that they step outside of their own comfort zones. Our ego doesn't like change either, and it doesn't like the feeling of being outside our comfort zone, which, as I've said before, is required if one is seeking a better life. Because of this, I wanted to provide a process for our ego to focus on so it wouldn't yell so loudly every time we even consider the idea of change. When we take change "one step at a time," our fear will actually be reduced and our odds for success will go up. My guide will help you move your focus off of the continual prattle of your inner fear voice and on to the steps of reinvention, which are far more interesting and helpful when it comes to improving your life!

Over the past three years, I developed and presented several versions of my ideas on raising awareness about our inner dynamic with money. The first workshop was titled *The Money Madness Cure*, which soon evolved into *My Money Shift*, and eventually into *Adventures in Money Mastery*. I see each version as a necessary step along my journey to understanding and developing a personal philosophy and effective program to teach women proven steps to help them transform their relationship with money and reinvent their life. I have spent thousands of hours researching, thinking, creating, writing, and ultimately testing my transformational philosophies and steps. The program that I am about to reveal to you has already helped many women and couples reinvent their lives. It holds the promise of helping thousands more in the future. The journey to this moment has been one of the most adventurous, thrilling, and joy-filled experiences of my life. I am honored to share the most current version of the steps that transformed my life and continue to transform the lives of my clients.

A STEP-BY-STEP MAP

My blueprint is a step-by-step map of the personal transformation journey—a structure that women can identify with and easily implement. Although there are many steps along the path to living your purpose and growing into your authentic self, the following seven phases can transform the journey from unapproachable to accessible. The goal of The Reinvention Blueprint™ is to provide you with a chart to successfully navigate the elements necessary to generate your dreams of a new life, to implement your intention to live your purpose, to reach your full potential, and to experience a joyful authentic life.

Most women in their late forties to early sixties have already reinvented themselves several times, but they may not be aware of the specific steps they took to do it. It took me over ten years to be able to draw a map of my own reinvention journey. Often, we reinvent ourselves out of necessity, when we experience normal life-changing events such as divorce, death of a spouse or other family member, having a baby, or quitting a job or career. These events act as catalysts that throw us into a state of questioning our lives and the choices we made in the past. Life events and aging changes us. Most would agree that the fifty-year-old woman we are now is very different from the thirty-year-old woman we were then. Midlife offers a perfect time to open ourselves up to the possibilities of living a different, more fulfilling, and meaningful life than the one we created twenty years ago and still inhabit. Many women are looking to create a life that fits better with the person they are now.

It's easy to understand how extreme life events push us into reinventing our lives and ourselves. However, there are also times in our lives when we become conscious that we just want to feel more, do more, and give more. We want to grow into someone new. We reach a point where we are willing to take a risk to change our lives, and do things that we wouldn't normally do to express who we are inside. The yearnings of our spirit to live our purpose and grow into our true authentic self become strong enough to kick us into action. That is when we look around for help. We look for a person to learn from, a guide to follow, and a process to help us through the inevitable bumps along the road. We seek a person who has experience and success at doing what we want to do—a person who has figured out the steps and wants to teach them to us. I have figured out those steps and here they are:

PHASE 1 — INVESTIGATE!

One way we stay stuck in life circumstances that we don't like is by pretending that our life is ok just the way it is. We convince ourselves that mediocrity is acceptable and that we really don't need or want a better life. We also tell ourselves that even if we wanted to have a different life, we just don't know how, or don't have the resources to create it. We trick ourselves into believing we have no options. This is not only limiting thinking, but belief viruses such as these can be hazardous to both our health and our happiness! An example would be the woman who stays with the abusive husband and convinces herself that it is her fault that he treats her the way he does. Another example would be the woman who continues to work as an executive assistant and expertly does her considerably higher paid bosses' job every day without seeking recognition in terms of pay and title for herself. We hide from the truth of who we are meant to become by working for less than our male counterparts and refusing to speak up for better treatment in our relationships. You can't begin to reinvent your life until you take an honest look at what is really happening in your life. Once you decide to use your gobs of courage to tell the truth, you will know where to start.

In this phase, we tell the truth about the real conditions of our life. We slow down the rat race that contributes to our false beliefs and examine the real facts of our financial condition, our relationships, our health, and our career. We ask hard questions so we can truly assess the quality of our life in order to determine if it is less than we deserve or desire. There is real power in accepting the truth about your life. When I was finally able to admit that I was addicted to shopping and an over spender, I had what I needed to be motivated to figure out how to stop the madness and get on with a better way of living my life. When you create the vision for your next chapter, you will feel such gratification as you realize just how far you have come, and how much closer you are to achieving your real life dreams. In this phase, we push the start button.

Reinvent You—INVESTIGATE!

Sit quietly by yourself and let your body and mind slow down. Drink a cup of chamomile tea and/or listen to soft music—breathe deeply. Once you feel more relaxed, ask your Higher Self to show you where you need to face the truth about yourself or a condition in your life that needs to be reinvented. Don't worry about how right now, just let the truth emerge and allow it to settle into your awareness and your body. If you realize a disturbing truth about yourself, be kind to yourself and allow any emotions that arrive to flow. Emotions that are invited for expression will flow through you like a wave and they will pass. Feel free to talk to a trusted friend or therapist if you feel it is necessary to process this experience.

PHASE 2—AWAKEN!

Once we identify and accept where we are in life, the question becomes how did we get here? Are there particular beliefs or habits that contributed to our current life situation? This question is critical to answer so limitations and roadblocks can be removed. In order to reinvent your life, you will need to become aware of the subconscious thinking and believing that has contributed to your situation. Many of our subconscious thoughts may actually help us along our journey so we won't need to discard everything. Here, we systematically separate thoughts and beliefs that are working for us from those that are not.

Human beings have a tendency to deny or reject certain memories, thoughts, or experiences because they were painful. We bury the pain we felt deep in our subconscious, mistakenly believing that if we bury it, we will never feel the pain again. Buried feelings come back to haunt us when something reminds us of the original event. An example from my life is that my father had a temper, and he would yell at me when he was unhappy about something I did. As an adult, every time someone raised their voice, I would be reminded of the fear and disempowerment that I felt as a child. I would freeze in place and be unable to think. This was one of the ways that domineering men were able to control me. Once I became aware of this dynamic in my life, I was able to heal it and bring forth my inner personal power so I could take steps to change my life for the better

When we invite our buried pain to come to the surface, and process the original experience that caused the pain, we can lessen its grip on our current behavior. When we let go of our past, we become free to move forward into the future we are yearning to live. We are so good at hiding our past pain that we create traps and circumstances that act as a sort of prison—conditions that we create but view as overwhelming and impossible to change. An example of a trap that we construct is the prison of financial scarcity. We use our lack of money as an excuse for not reaching for more in our lives. Financial scarcity is created only by repeating the same limiting actions over and over. There is no such thing as scarcity. I know it may trigger a negative response just to read those words, but I invite you to be open to the possibility that it might be true. Once we wake up to how we limit and stop ourselves, as well as remember who we really are inside, hope for a better future transforms to an inner confidence that everything we dream of is truly within our reach. In this phase, we awaken our awareness to the limitations that block us from achieving our dreams, and process them in order to loosen their grip on our lives.

Reinvent You—AWAKEN!

Consider an area of your life that is not working as well as you would like it to right now. Perhaps your job is frustrating or you haven't had a date for over three years. Whatever is happening in your life, for this exercise, do the best you can to take 100% responsibility for the situation. I don't want you to blame or beat yourself up, but I want you to see this condition from the viewpoint that you have all the power to do something about it. Once you try on that perspective, you can explore what contributes to the situation. If your job is frustrating, perhaps you are walking around angry all the time, or you tell everyone you aren't appreciated. Do the best you can to focus in on your behavior and then do a little self-analysis. Was your mother angry a lot when you were growing up? Did you do a lot of chores around the house and were never thanked? See if you can connect the dots between your conditions, how you behave in those conditions, and how they might tie into your past. Once you identify the memory or event that created your current beliefs and behavior, then you have everything you need to heal it and let it go! This can be tricky, which is why it helps to have a coach, but give it a try. You might have a huge aha moment about yourself that improves the situation immediately.

PHASE 3—LIBERATE!

When we uncover the truth about conditions that keep us stuck in our current life situation, we have a choice. We can either stay in the comfort zone of those conditions or step outside our comfort zone in order to clear them up and let them go. This is where we learn how to liberate ourselves from the chains that bind us to a small and unhappy life. In this phase, we acknowledge that everything we want is outside our comfort zone, and if we want it bad enough, we have to grow ourselves into the person we need to become when our dreams show up. How liberating is that? Once you identify unconscious thoughts and beliefs, process them, and let go of the events that created them, you feel empowered to create new thought patterns that support your inner purpose and dreams for your future! Liberation occurs when we stop saying no to ourselves in order to stay safe, and start saying yes to ourselves in order to grow. We need to work on shifting our entire attitude about what is truly possible for us, in this life at this time. We begin learning to inhabit the knowing that we indeed have everything it takes already inside of us to reach our full potential. In this phase, we liberate and renew our energy and prepare a new foundation of thoughts and beliefs for the journey ahead.

Reinvent You—LIBERATE!

Take the condition you identified in the Awaken exercise and see if you can become aware of your thoughts around your behavior. If you are unhappy at work and have realized it's because you are angry all the time, see if you can pick out one negative thought that you have all the time. Perhaps you think "My boss treats me like a child" when you interact with him/her. If you think that thought habitually every day, no wonder you are angry! See if you can turn your negative thought into a new, more positive thought. Instead of thinking "My boss treats me like a child," you could think, "No matter how my boss treats me, I am a highly functioning adult with great ideas and a good work ethic." There are more steps to turning your negative thinking into positive thinking, but hopefully this will give you a taste of how liberating it can be when you take steps to turn your thoughts into supportive habits of thinking in order to reinvent your work life!

PHASE 4 — CO-CREATE!

Here we explore the essence of Her and our connection to our co-creative Higher Power. We strengthen our intuition and explore the realities of how our mind, body, and spirit interact when filled with passion and purpose. We identify different voices in our head—the ego voice and the voice of our authentic self—and learn how to allow each voice to work with us, not stop us, as we journey toward our authentic life. We design daily rituals to strengthen our connection to creative forces and spiritual laws. Meditation, prayer, gratitude, and spending time in nature are proven tools that will help us move forward on our quest. We prepare the soil for the next phase by learning to listen to our heart as well as our head. We begin to embody who we truly are and practice living a spiritually connected life.

Reinvent You — CO-CREATE!

Carve out five minutes in the morning and five minutes before you go to sleep as "me" time. Commit to spending this time alone in a place where you can relax and reflect. Close your eyes and place your awareness on your breath. Take several deep breaths to begin the relaxation process and let go of the stress. Once you are feeling more relaxed, continue to follow your breath. Place your focus on different parts of your body. Notice anything you may sense in your body as you breathe. Become aware of any thoughts that come into your mind. Be mindful of your emotions. Allow what you feel and think to come into your awareness and leave your awareness without stopping or reacting to it. When you are ready to move on, open your eyes. Write down in your journal what you became aware of. When we slow down and allow our inner gifts—our mind, our emotions, our intuition, and our Higher Power—to speak to us, we have the opportunity to receive valuable wisdom. I invite you to make this a daily priority; however, there is no need to feel guilty if you miss a day. Allow this time to be a gift you give yourself, not something you have to do. Give yourself permission to let it flow naturally.

PHASE 5—ENVISION!

Now that our connection to our inner spirit and Higher Power are established, we are ready to envision how our next chapter will unfold. I describe visualizing your dream life as if you were making a movie in your mind of the best life you can envision now. We explore possibilities of our life purpose and how we might manifest our vision realistically at this time of our life. We borrow from Jack Canfield's book *The Success Principles*, and consider our dream life in seven life categories, including career, relationships, finances, health, fun, personal, and legacy. We visualize what a balanced life would look like for us if nothing were in the way of its creation. Once we visualize our dream life, we choose which area of our life to focus on first.

The next step is to set goals and action steps deigned to take us closer to our goal every day. We establish a daily habit of visualization, goal statements, and action steps—all designed to attract and manifest our new life. In this phase, we open up to looking for synchronistic events and practice living in the flow of divine co-creation.

Reinvent You—ENVISION!

My experience with reinvention has proven that once you reinvent one area of your life, you can reinvent any and all areas of your life. Go ahead and expand the question that you asked yourself at the end of Chapter IV. Write down what you want in your work and career, your relationships, your finances, your personal life, your health and fitness, your fun and recreation, and your legacy. Create a list that you continue to add to as you live your life. Don't worry if you don't answer with a long list in the beginning. The more you ask the question, the more your inner spirit and Higher Power will present you with exciting and spectacular alternatives. Expand your thinking into what's possible for you. Once you have considered the possibilities, you can start making choices.

PHASE 6—ACTIVATE!

Our dreams come true by not only visualizing, believing, and working in harmony with our inner and Higher Power, but also by taking inspired and empowered action. We use the power of our mind and our ability to set powerful intentions in order to achieve written and measurable goals. We use our new energy to take massive action every day to lead us closer to our vision. We continue to rely on a positive mindset to fuel our belief that miracles can and do happen. We give our vision even more power to manifest by working with an accountability partner, someone who we report the progress on our actions, and who will support and encourage us to continue our journey during inevitable hard times. We join or create a synergistic group of like-minded peers to provide fellowship, creative ideas, love, support, and celebration along our journey.

Reinvent You—ACTIVATE!

Look over the lists of what you want and pick one that really motivates you. Think about a first action step you could take to start the process of getting what you say you want. Perhaps you want to change the direction of your career. You are working in healthcare, and you've always dreamed of owning a bakery. One first step might be to visit a bakery that you like and talk to the owner about what it took for her to get started. Another first step might be to make your favorite chocolate cake recipes and invite ten people over to sample them and give you feedback. Once you start taking action on your dreams, you feel empowered to take the next and the next. Reinvention happens when you take your dreams and make them a reality by taking action one step at a time!

PHASE 7—EVOLVE!

The Reinvention Journey is a life-long voyage. Wherever we are along the journey, and whatever new chapter we are creating in our life now, as long as we continue to integrate The Reinvention Blueprint™ in our lives, we will continue to achieve higher and higher states of spiritual awareness, financial success, unconditional love, and profound happiness and joy in our lives. The success of a long-term personal development path requires a commitment to daily meditation, gratitude, and self-love rituals; healthy eating and exercise; spiritual enrichment and ongoing support; accountability and coaching.

Walking the path of reinvention is a one-step-at-a-time process, but it is not designed to be inflexible or limiting. I invite everyone who engages the journey to put their own personal stamp and preferences on the reinvention process. Reinvention is always growing and expanding, and I welcome new ideas and contributions to make the journey more inviting to more women. Learning to make the process your own will increase the odds that you will keep going, that you will establish "reaching my full potential" as a lifetime goal that you will not compromise on. The idea of reinventing one's entire life can feel overwhelming which can stop us from even getting started. I encourage you to focus on just one area of your life in the beginning. As I've mentioned before, when you learn how to reinvent one area of your life, you can use the same methods and experience to reinvent any or all areas of your life.

Since I am a financial planner, many women hire me to help them change their relationship with money, although I also coach women in all life reinvention areas as well. If a major life transformation is on your mind, you will need to reinvent your relationship with money at some point along the way. You can start with money or end with money. It's entirely up to you to pick the order of your personal reinvention. What truly matters to me is that you feel empowered to reinvent, or improve any or all parts of your life. I designed the blueprint to give you as much direction and support that you personally need to win.

Reinvent You—EVOLVE!

 Congratulations! If you have completed all the exercises in this book, you have already increased your awareness and expanded what's possible for your life. What will you do now? Based on research on how much we retain when learning, called the Learning Pyramid, it is estimated that we retain as much as 50% of what we learn if we discuss the material. We retain 75% of what we learn when we practice it and 90% of what we learn when we teach it to others. Now you know why I wrote this book. How much of what you learned do you wish to retain? What will you do to make that happen?

I am committed to helping women reinvent their lives in order to be happier, more authentic, more purposeful, and filled with exquisite joy. I invite you to engage The Reinvention Blueprint™ in your life. Visit **www.ReinventionBlueprint.com** to find out the options available to you so you can get started on your personal reinvention journey.

SALLY'S LIFE REINVENTION

Sally hurried home from her coffee appointment with her best friend Jill. She was in a rush to get home so she could tear open the envelope holding the application documents to adopt a child that she had been staring at, unopened, for over two weeks. Jill's last words were still ringing in her ears, "Nobody can afford a child when they have one, Sally. If we all waited until we could afford children, we would never have them!"

This had been the last fear holding Sally back from opening that envelope and starting the process to achieve her most precious dream, to adopt a child. Only six months out from surviving breast cancer, Sally was highly motivated to live her dream of becoming a mom. "I didn't have to be a genius to realize I was given a second chance in life. Suddenly, I was filled with an urgency to get going on creating my life the way I wanted to live it!" Sally explained.

Sally had applied to adopt a child in the United States and a few other countries as a single adoptive mother. Being single didn't seem to be a hurdle, but being a breast cancer survivor was. After multiple rejections, suddenly and unexpectedly, she was given a green light from Guatemala. "As long as my doctor signed a letter that my cancer was in remission, they assured me my application would be fully considered," she said.

Once she actually decided to take action on her dream of adopting a child, Sally's fears came tumbling out. How would she handle childcare, balance a full-time job while raising a child, and the biggest fear of all, how would she be able to afford it?

"I didn't know anything about adoption. No one in my family had ever adopted before, and I especially knew nothing about adopting a foreign-born child. I was terrified that I would do it wrong, that it would cost me more money than I had set aside, and that after months, or even years of trying, I wouldn't have a child. Once I made up my mind, I knew I would just have to jump and trust that everything would work out," she added.

Trust is what she did and she was immediately rewarded by a series of synchronistic events. "I just kept trusting that it would happen, that all I had to do was hold my intention and follow the steps outlined in front of me. My friends and family would say, 'Don't get your hopes up,' and I told them, 'Don't worry. It's going to happen. I know it in my heart,'" she shared.

Sally believed so completely that her child was on the way, that she finished her application in record time. She turned it in on a Friday and the very next Monday she received a call. "I thought it was a call to check or correct something on my application, but it was the call that I didn't expect to get for months. 'We have a little girl for you,' the representative said. Those words were the sweetest words I had ever heard," Sally told me. There were other families ahead of her on the adoption waiting list, but they all had different reasons for passing on this little girl. "It was meant to be. I knew it when I saw her picture that she was my daughter. It was instant and it was clear."

Then, Sally focused her attention on bringing her daughter home before she was one year old. "Most adopted children come home older than a year, but the adoption doors were closing in Guatemala so I knew my daughter would have to be home before she was a year old in order to be sure to meet the deadline." Sally had a strong belief that they would make it before the deadline, and they did. Her daughter came home at eight months old. "People said, 'How lucky for you!' but I knew it wasn't luck. It was my strong intention and belief that created the circumstances for her to be home," she explained.

USING THE BLUEPRINT TO REINVENT HER LIFE

Many women are motivated to reinvent their lives after a major life event. For Sally, it was surviving cancer. Her adoption experience proved to her that there was a powerful force available for her to tap into. Now that she had a child, she was anxious to turn her attention to reinventing other areas of her life.

I met Sally when her daughter was five years old. She told me she was highly motivated to take more steps toward living an authentic and happy life. "Before I had cancer I was very passive and let things happen to me. I had a 'this is better than nothing' attitude. Now I consciously and whole-heartedly know that I create my life. I want to make different choices, actively choose whom I spend time with, and what I want to have happen in my life. I want to open up to the possibilities so I won't miss out on the best life my daughter and I can have," she said.

Sally had always been proactive with her career and expertly designed a profession that many women would envy. She realized she didn't have the same confidence when it came to financial management or personal relationships. She knew that if she was going to achieve her dream life, she would need assistance to reinvent those two areas. "I never tracked where I was financially. I managed money the way I did the rest of my life, just letting things happen to me. Once my daughter came home, I realized I couldn't wing it anymore. I now wanted a system, a way to make sure I was providing us everything we would need and want as she grew up," she said.

Similar to other women who believe they don't have the knowledge, or aren't smart enough to create real financial security, Sally didn't trust herself to make good financial decisions. Together, we explored the source of her lack of confidence. During *Phase I—Investigate* she was surprised to learn that her lack of confidence came from a belief that she was "not enough." She developed this mistaken belief during childhood. "My parents were awesome growing up, but I remember that most of the messages I received were based on their fears for

me. 'You shouldn't take that risk' or 'That's not going to work out' was their constant refrain. My parents were trying to protect me, but the message I got was that they didn't believe in me. Since they didn't believe in me, I didn't believe in me," she said.

Sally used her gobs of courage and continued to explore and process other limiting beliefs around money. She told me that our conversations and processing motivated her to read dozens of self-help and personal development books. She attended seminars, workshops, hired other coaches, and learned to trust that each new teacher would have the message that she was ready to hear. "I opened myself up to teachers, because I really wanted to learn how 'this stuff' works. I watched people who were living their new beliefs, people like you who were bravely taking steps to manifest a new life. That was very powerful for me," she said. "It helped me to keep going even when I was confused and feeling defeated. My parents kept telling me that I was crazy, but I wanted to show them that once I set my mind to something, that I would do anything to make it happen."

One of the hardest things that Sally had to give up was the belief that she could control the "how" in her life evolution. By learning how much she was limiting her life by not believing in herself, she made a commitment to change her inner belief to one of complete and total belief in herself. "You have to believe that everything will show up when it is meant to, when you are ready for it," said Sally. "You have to believe that you have everything you need to attract what you want and that you deserve to live the life of your choosing."

In Phase 4, Sally began to understand the co-creative connection with her Higher Power. As she established a daily meditation habit, she began to visualize a new direction for work. "At first, I thought I wanted to help women recovering from cancer and I was satisfied with the thought of making a minimal impact as a private coach," she added. "Now my vision is much bigger and I'm no longer afraid to go for it!" Working with teachers and mentors contributed to the development of her strong belief in herself, and her connection to Spirit has reduced her fear of failure and of the risks she will have to take to achieve her big dream. "I immersed myself and continued to read, study, and attend workshops until I achieved the confidence and vision that I hoped for."

Sally is making progress toward achieving her vision and one of the most important aspects of achieving it will be managing her financial life. She realized that this is not her strength, nor is she interested in spending the time necessary to learn the technical side of financial decision-making. "What you give me is the confidence that I *can* create my life with the support of my money. Now that I have an advisor,

I am free to trust that together we will develop and follow a plan designed to meet my life goals."

Sally added, "My relationship with money has changed because I changed myself. I am more creative and I am open to different options. I tell people that when you change yourself inside, your outside results will change. That is what happened to me. I have different emotional reactions to things that happen in my life and even that small difference has made a huge impact on how happy I am. The results in my life are surprisingly different, and I know that I am on the journey to a more rewarding and happy life."

Bill and Bethann, Ellen, Mandy, and Sally are happily living their versions of reinvention. If they were here in front of you and you asked them for advice, I think they would urge you to get started. They wouldn't tell you that reinvention is easy, or that it doesn't have its ups and downs, but what they would tell you is that it is worth it—so worth it. Their lives are now full of adventure, positive experiences, connection, and accomplishment. Their lives are bigger and more beautiful and they know who they are and they *like* themselves. They would tell you they are grateful to be on their journey.

EPILOGUE

*S*o here we are together at the end of this book. If you are still with me, I am grateful, and I applaud you for your willingness to be open and to see what this book could offer you— all the way to the end.

As I said in the beginning, I wrote this book as an invitation to you; an invitation to reinvent your life, an invitation to make your life the best one it can possibly be. I've shared how I reinvented my life into the best it could possibly be, at least up to this point. I've shared my philosophy, as well as five Reinvention Pillars, in hopes that you could really understand what it takes to alter yourself and improve your life for the better. I've designed a step-by-step process, **The Reinvention Blueprint**™ to help you focus on steps that have been proven to help others reinvent their lives. I truly want you to understand the inner workings of reinvention and know that it is not impossible. It's just the opposite. It's simple and achievable!

I've been as honest as I could about the challenges and hard work that is required to reinvent your life. I haven't pretended that it's a bed of roses because it isn't. It's the hardest work you will ever do, but also the most rewarding. Reinventing your life offers the chance to actually take those dreams out of your head and make them a reality. I offered a glimpse into the lives of real women who are successfully using my system to improve their lives. Hopefully I've motivated you to start your reinvention journey and make it a lifelong commitment. If you do decide to begin your journey, you will notice improvements right away, even if the big changes you are hoping to manifest take more time to arrive.

It's not easy to wait for the big changes to occur. It's not easy to go to work every day at a job you don't enjoy while you take the small action steps necessary to start your own business. It's not easy to get on the scales and see you've only lost a pound when your goal is to lose one hundred. The daily steps needed to create the life you desire requires a strong commitment and gobs of courage. But every time you succeed in going to the gym, or saying no to chocolate cake, or spend an hour on your website copy, you can smile inside, feel that sweet sense of accomplishment, and settle into that inner knowing that you are going to make it. The small steps of growth you make on the inside every day will sustain your motivation and excitement as you take action on the long-term vision for your new life. Practicing new awareness techniques, changing beliefs that no longer serve you, establishing new positive habits—those are the pieces of reinvention that will sustain and grow you so that you will be the person you need to be when your big dreams arrive.

Writing this book has been a major focus for me for over four years. In order to arrive in this moment, I had to allow my individual voice to come out and let go of limiting beliefs and fears that I wasn't "enough" to write a book. I had to square my shoulders and speak my truth, even though I was afraid that some people might judge me or disagree with me. I'm just like you. I want to be liked, and I am hurt every single time someone rejects me. I still feel pain, but I don't let it stop me from reinventing my life.

I wanted the book to go faster, to be easier, to flow out of me naturally with divine grace. Some parts of the book were actually created from divine flow, while others felt more like a birth by C-section. My reinvention is just like yours—beautiful, reward-  ing, frustrating, painful, and wonderful. I wouldn't stop reinventing myself for all the money in the world, and once you begin your reinvention journey, I believe you won't either.

I was surprised by how much emotion I felt when writing the section on excavating Her. I have experienced deep pain in my life and I have watched and listened to other women express theirs. And I am very committed to helping women reduce the amount of pain that they live with every day. Whenever I speak to a woman on the phone and hear how she gives up her power—at work, at home, with her health, or how she lets others hurt her—I want to cry. Sometimes I do cry. "How can I get her attention," I think. "How can I snap her out of it?" It's all I want to do—help you and all other women who are stuck in pain. I want to help you wake up to the truth that your life doesn't have to be as difficult as you are making it. You just have to wake up. Wake up. Please.

Your life will change on the outside when you are willing to change on the inside. Your pain will subside when you are willing to accept that you are a powerful woman and that you have what you need to live a much better life. Remember, you can't live a positive life from a negative thought. The first step is to stop thinking so negatively and to stop beating yourself up. Become aware of your negative thinking and turn it around to positive thinking. Yes, it takes time and effort to do this in the beginning, but just like anything, over time you can form a new, positive habit, and when you do, your life will get easier. Your life will transform in so many great ways that you will start kicking up your heels and laughing and jumping and feeling glorious.

Your life will evolve when you disconnect from the belief viruses that infect you and the rest of our culture, and choose to walk through the door to freedom. There are so many of us over here on the other side of the door, doing the best we can to live our truth and find our purpose, and we will welcome you with open arms. We will hold you and love you and help you through the first few awkward steps of your personal reinvention. Once you get started, you will find your pace and your reinvention will pick up speed. It's just like riding a bike—a little rough at first, but once you know how to do it, you'll never fall off again.

Those of us who are already living the reinvention journey are here to support you, to listen to you, to motivate you. We are here for you and to remind you of all the beautiful gifts that you carry inside. We already see Her in all of her glory and wisdom and will empower you to let her lead, to let her guide your future growth. She is your intuition, your love, your passion, and your femininity. Your birth as a woman was an invitation to experience this life through her eyes—to learn and grow and shine as the very essence of goddess divinity. Regardless of what you believe right now, you can bring her to work, to the gym, to your in-laws for dinner, or to your volunteer job at the hospital. Your friends and family might be a little taken aback at first, but they will grow to love her very quickly. Trust her. When you invite Her to play a larger role in your life, when you confidently allow her to touch you, to teach you, to love you, the magic of your life will surprise and delight you in every way. Your life will be exquisitely joyful when you allow your beautiful spirit to walk freely in the material world.

You are the Venus of our time. You and every other woman are the goddesses of love, of birth, and of the natural flow of life and its creation. You are here. We are here, in this time and place, to heal the world with our powerful goddess love. This is our purpose—to allow our inner Venus to come out so she can love and heal the world. You are the answer to your own prayers. You are the gift the world needs now.

At a 2009 Vancouver Peace Summit, the Dalai Lama said something that surprised the world. He said that he is a feminist and that Western women will save the world. Let that sink in for a moment. Are you a Western woman? I believe he said that because, in general, women who live in the West are more empowered to lead and to act from their inner power than women in the East. We need powerful women who have remembered who they are, who have embraced their purpose, and who have made a commitment to heal the world. We need these higher consciousness women to move to the front of the line. Our world and its people desperately need us now, and we may be running short of time. Every single woman alive today has a role to play in the healing of the world and our job is to figure out what our role is. It may not resonate for you to become another Oprah, or Hillary Clinton, or Janet Yellen, but there is a place for you to make a difference. Are you ready to make a difference?

You have an important role to play. You have a difference to make. There is no contribution that is too small. If you motivate even one person to stop smoking, to stop watching violent movies, or to volunteer their time at a local homeless shelter, then you have done your part. Reinvent your life to one that includes doing your part and making the difference you are meant to make. Get started on figuring out what that difference is and what your verse of the world's song is that you are meant to sing. The journey to finding it is really fun! It is so much more entertaining than playing victim and complaining about your boss and numbing yourself out with mindless TV every night. Your own life can be the movie you watch and this time you become the star! It can even be a comedy if that's what you want; you are the one making the movie! Make the movie of your amazing life. It's what you were put here to do.

Remember who you really are. Trust your inner gifts and allow your beautiful spirit to walk on the earth. Unhook from the fear-based belief viruses. Repair your "wanter" and empower yourself to desire things again. Tell the truth faster and divorce your money, and remember money is a tool that was designed to help you make your dreams come true. Stop "should" living and put your dreams at the top of your list.

Love Her and respect Her and reinvent Her. Find your way to love and heal the world.

With deep love and gratitude,

Tresa Leftenant

ACKNOWLEDGEMENTS

*H*ow many times have you read a book and thought to yourself, "There is no way that many people had something to do with this book?" I have thought the same thing, and yet, here I am about to thank the entire world for every gift and kind word that I've ever received. Attempting this herculean task feels daunting, because I don't want to leave anyone out, and I don't know whom to thank first! I guess I'll follow my own advice and do it one step at a time

It takes a village to write a book and assembling the right team can be the difference between a good day and a bad month. What I know for sure is that I wouldn't have even attempted to write a book without my writing coach Kathy Sparrow. Her passion for helping neophyte authors get their inner passion out of their head and onto the page is nothing short of amazing. With a perfect blend of coaching, guiding, cheerleading, and parenting, Kathy coaxed my baby out of the womb. I will be forever in her debt and am grateful for her patience and unwavering belief in me. We actually had a little fun too, which I will always remember fondly. My design and editing team—Beth Fountain and Jennifer Carter are professionals that any writer would be grateful to have—thank you for your creativity and willingness to jump on a train that was already moving at light speed.

Thank you to my dear female friends, my ladies discussion group, and especially the women who agreed to read my book in a weekend and provide me with valuable feedback that informed this final printed version. Writing a book is a lonely excursion—it's only my thoughts, my computer, and me. Every author wonders if their story and wisdom, as well as the time committed, will be of any use or will be seen as a contribution. Your enthusiasm and your expressive words of awe and respect for this book filled me with a knowing that my purpose had been met. There is no greater satisfaction than to be understood. What you think of me is none of my business, but hearing how well my gifts were being received gave me a heady feeling. I am empowered by it and grateful that I did not keep those gifts, but let them fade away, lest my ego believe that they are more than just an opinion and that they are part of who I am. Thank you to Cindy, Michelle, Marilyn, Rose, Paula, and Lili for your support, friendship, and unconditional love. A special thank you to Sally Huss—I am honored to receive a review from a woman who has lived the very essence of reinvention.

My Higher Power has always been looking out for me, never more lovingly than last fall when I met Eileen Gordon. She took one look at me and asked why I was content playing my "B" game. She then went on to succinctly—and expertly—draw out my "A" game and challenge me to stop wasting my gifts and move forward in giving them. Once you face the truth, you can never un-know it; it becomes a fact that must be lived. Creating a movement around women transforming into their full potential became a day and night obsession overnight. The wisdom and knowledge inside this book was perfectly ripe and all that was needed was the right person to give me permission to share it. Thank you for your particular gift of listening to a thought and transforming it into a **big** idea. Your extraordinary genius is the ability to combine your intuition, raw talent, and unrivaled skill to reinvent an idea into a theme and a theme into a movement. Your ability to masterfully craft a concept, a guiding principal into one that lands deep in the heart of the reader, the listener, the soul of anyone fortunate enough to be open to absorb it. I am in awe of your passion for empowering others and not taking one bit of credit for yourself. You put everything on the line and give everything you have, every time you get on the phone. You are my inspiration and I am honored to share your gifts through my work as we both follow our calling to change and heal the world. Thank you to Eileen's team—Ken Preuss for your unique ability to refine a concept, and Amanda for the beautiful cover artwork, website, and brand that I am truly proud of.

To celebrity photographer Doug Ellis, your willingness to meet me in Malibu on the one day I was in Los Angeles was truly an amazing and huge gift. Our day at Getty Villa was divinely arranged and you have the perfect eye for just the right light and just the right smile. Blessings, my friend—I will forever be your loyal subject.

My personal reinvention story is guided by coaches and trainers whom I respect, admire, and attempt to emulate in my own coaching and advisory practice. My angel, Sue Wade, introduced me to the concept of self-esteem and gently urged my children and me to follow the path to self-assurance and self-love. Your dedication and belief in us has paid off, sweet friend. Thank you to the unsung heroines of my experiential trainings—Sylvia Badasci, Eleanor Hanauer, Krista Petty, and Susan Kenny. Your particular brand of tough love was what I needed in order to let go of my victim thinking and step forward into responsible living. I know how incredibly lucky I was to be in that time and place, and to receive the gifts given in those trainings. There isn't a day that goes by where I don't thank you for a miraculous life skill that I am presently using to more successfully navigate my life. Namaste, my angels.

To my mentor Jack Canfield, who has dedicated his life to filling as many hearts and minds with the concepts of self-love, self-empowerment, and spiritual connection as he can. When I think of you, I wonder if there will ever be enough thank you's to communicate how grateful I am for the influence you and your work has had in my life. Seeing your face in my mind and considering what to say fills my entire body with gratitude and I realize that is exactly what you want. It's living from gratitude and passing it on that is the ultimate acknowledgement to you. So know that I am filled with my own version of purpose, that your message of love and healing has been received, and that I am paying it forward to any and all who come my way. All my love, Jack.

Many parents agree the most rewarding and life-affirming experience is that of having a child. My life is blessed with two incredible spirits who came through my body to live on this earth. They are such fascinating and amazing people that it is hard to remember they are not mine. Yes, I did bear them, but only to help them learn a few lessons before they flew off to live their own version of a life. My most cherished life memories were experienced during those few short years of living and learning together. Gina and Graham, you fill me with pride, and my heart overflows with love whenever I see you or think of you. You are the light and the blessing of my life and everything is worth it because of you. My blessing of children doubled when I married Gordon and met his incredible daughter, Alexis. You completed our family and I have loved every minute watching you grow and express your gifts in the world.

One day, during a training event, I noticed a tall brown man across the room. I remember my mind and body stopped and I gazed over at him, completely overwhelmed with curiosity and amazement. A few months later, that same man saw me across the same room and had a similar experience. "Who is that?" he asked his companion. Several months later, we both walked around a picnic table and found ourselves face to face with one another. "Hello," we both said out loud. A conversation ensued and as we both later reported, it was deep and meaningful and unforgettable. Even more months went by and I found myself at an event raising money for a charity by auctioning off dates with bachelors and bachelorettes. The brown man found himself there too and before we knew it, he had purchased a date with a particular bachelorette, which happened to be me. The details of the evening make a pretty good story, but the point of the story is that two people, who were meant to be together, found each other that evening. From that night on, we have loved each other fiercely and created a life and a marriage that far surpasses anything we could have ever dreamed up.

On the day of our marriage, a short five months after our first date, we vowed to create a family that we designed, that met our needs and not the expectations of others. We vowed to continue to grow into the people we were meant to become, and that supporting each other's growth, as well as our children's, would be our top priority. Fifteen years later, we have lived our commitment to each other and by doing so have broken new ground of intimacy and closeness. This is not the first marriage for either of us, but it is by far the best marriage for both of us. We met after we had both survived the fires of relationship dishonesty, and had suffered the pain of disloyalty and disrespect. Our relationship provides me with the solid foundation from which to reinvent myself and test my philosophy and program that I teach in this book. Without the love of my dear and beautiful husband, I suspect I would not be writing these words today. Nor would I have had the exquisitely joyful life that I have been privileged to live. Thank you my life, my love, my wonderful Gordon, for lifting me up and never letting me fall.

Your Next Chapter: The Eight Powerful Secrets of a Life Reinvention

IN THIS FREE EXPERIENTIAL E-COURSE, YOU WILL LEARN:

- Why desire is the doorway to reinvention...
  and how to tap into your own inner desires

- How to get out of your brain and into your body to
  learn who you really are

- Why you aren't quite ready for things you want...
  and how to get ready faster

- Why reinvention hasn't happened to you yet (hint:
  you are holding yourself where you are right now)

- The #1 transformative thought about money
  (it's not what you think)

- Three powerful strategies for making change easier

- Why reinventing only one area of your life actually
  begins the reinvention of your entire life

- The true starting point of all reinvention... and how
  to access it yourself

HTTP://WWW.REINVENTINGHER.COM/FREECOURSE

FROM THE AUTHOR

*T*he first time I heard the word "reinvention," I thought it was one of those new age words that certain people used to convince other people they knew more about how to live a happy life. Back then, I was running on life's treadmill full force as a mother of two kids and an assistant vice president of a regional bank. I didn't have a shred of interest in changing my life, and I cringed when I heard spiritual psychobabble like "life is a journey" and "connect to your Higher Power." Who has time for that?!

I'm not going to pull any punches about who I used to be. Before my personal reinvention, I was a self-loathing victim. I settled for abusive, co-dependent relationships with men who had no direction in life. I had limited life skills and no college education. I lived a "Jerry Springer life" chock full of three-martini lunches, an over-the-top shopping addiction, and multiple infidelities. All the while, I criticized family members and acquaintances for living a "trailer trash" life. Looking back, I had very little to be proud of.

My personal reinvention is the drive behind Reinventing Her. It is not only my passion to pass on what I've learned—it is also my responsibility. There is no way I could even think about helping you reinvent your life had I not done the work in my own life. When I reinvented my finances, I began speaking to groups about changing their results and relationship to money. That started nearly fifteen years ago. Since then, I honed my skills and my philosophy. I laid out the exact steps I used to reinvent the areas of money, relationships, career, health, and spirituality into what I now call **The Reinvention Blueprint**.™ Today, I am in a romance-novel relationship with Gordon, my current husband of fifteen years. I continue to support our children's reinvention. My daughter is a physician, my son is a budding film producer, and Gordon's daughter is a music composer. I started my own financial planning practice eleven years ago and built it into a multi six-figure income success. I dropped twenty-five pounds and established a healthy eating regimen. I own two homes, I travel whenever I want, and gratefully enjoy an abundant lifestyle. I can tell you for sure that none of this was "in the cards" fifteen years ago.

For more information and to start your reinvention journey, visit www.reinventingher.com.

Tresa Leftenant is a licensed financial advisor with LPL Financial. Securities and advisory services offered through LPL Financial, a registered investment advisor. Member FINRA/SIPC. For a list of states where Tresa is registered to do business, please visit www.myfinancialdesign.com.

Certified Financial Planner Board of Standards Inc. owns the certification marks CFPR and CERTIFIED FINANCIAL PLANNER in the U.S., which it awards to individuals who successfully complete CFP Board's initial and ongoingcertification requirements. See more at: http://www.cfp.net/

CPSIA information can be obtained
at www.ICGtesting.com
Printed in the USA
FFOW04n1717170518
46722753-48862FF